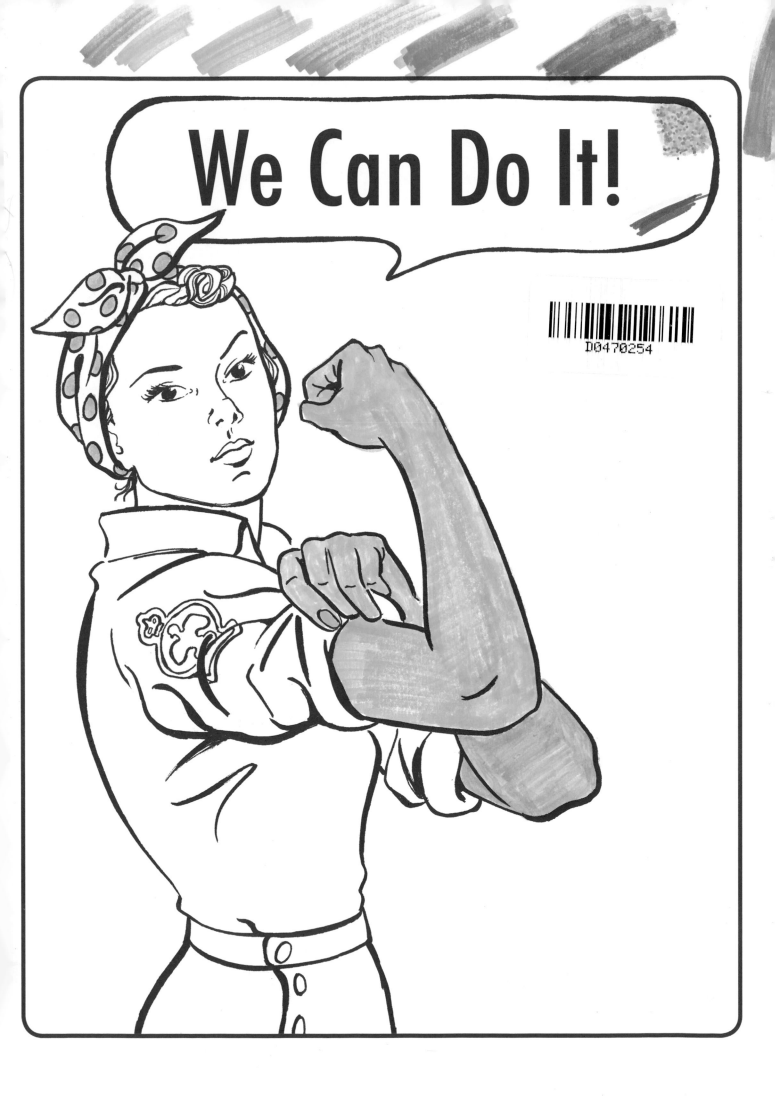

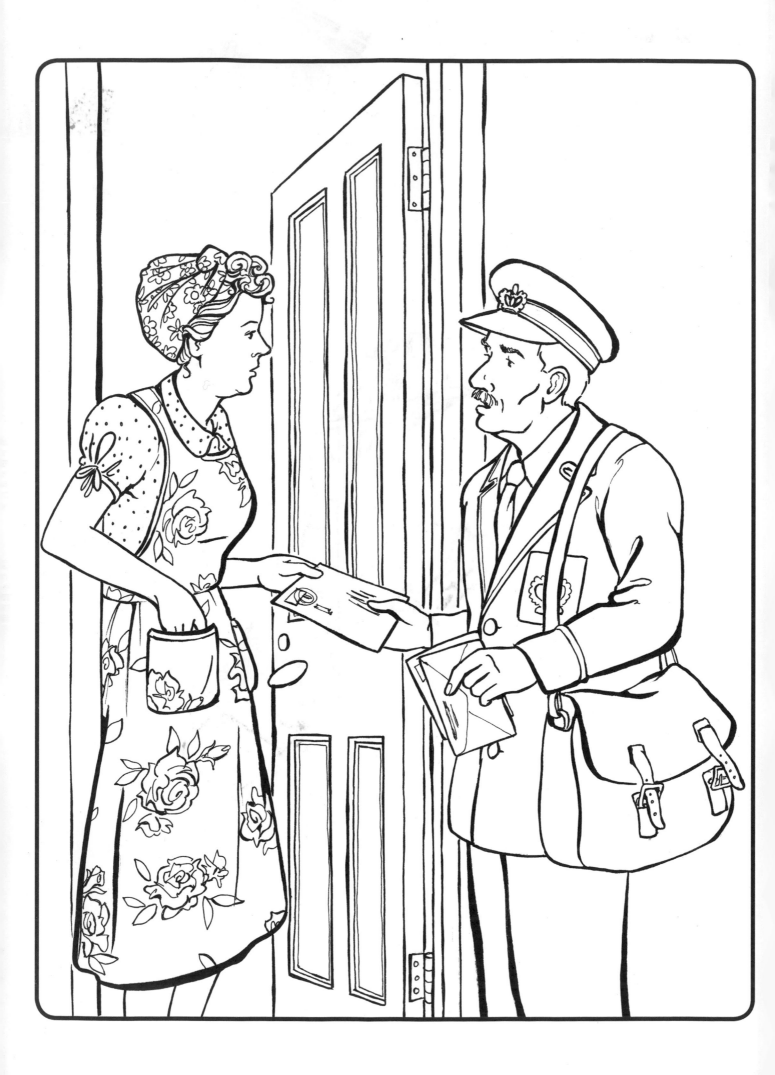

KEEP CALM AND COLOUR IN

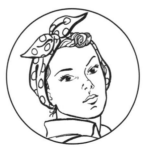

A 1940s COLOURING BOOK

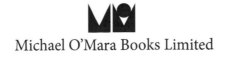

Michael O'Mara Books Limited

First published in Great Britain in 2013 by
Michael O'Mara Books Limited
9 Lion Yard
Tremadoc Road
London SW4 7NQ

A CIP catalogue record for this book is available from the British Library.

Papers used by Michael O'Mara Books Limited are natural, recyclable products made from wood grown in sustainable forests. The manufacturing processes conform to the environmental regulations of the country of origin.

ISBN: 978-1-78243-154-1

1 2 3 4 5 6 7 8 9 10

www.mombooks.com

Illustrations by Ann Kronheimer and Virginia Gray

Designed by Ana Bjezancevic

Printed and bound in China

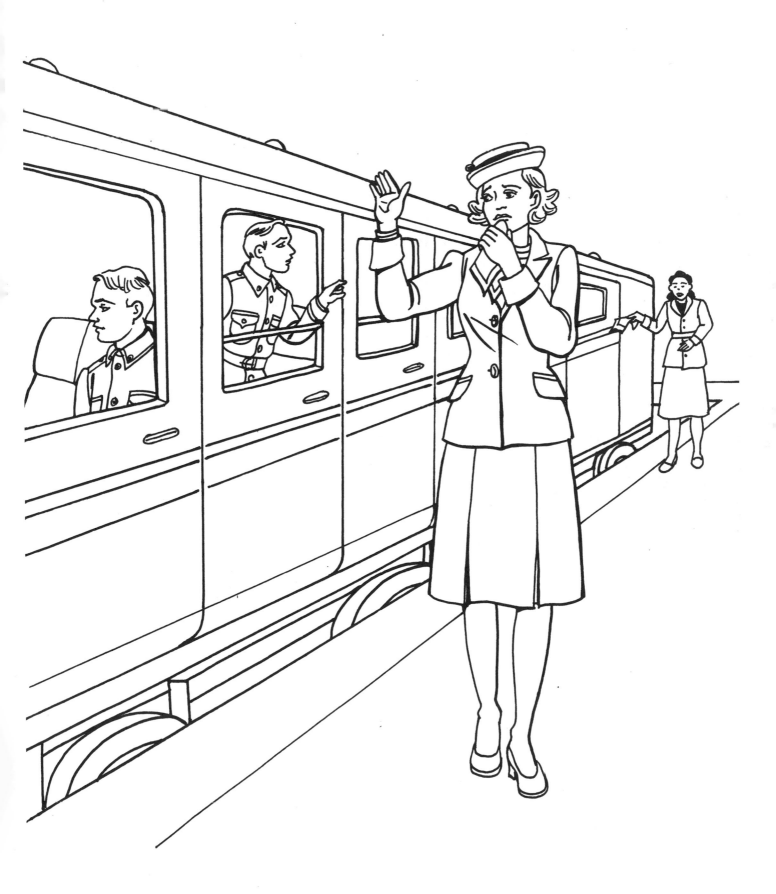

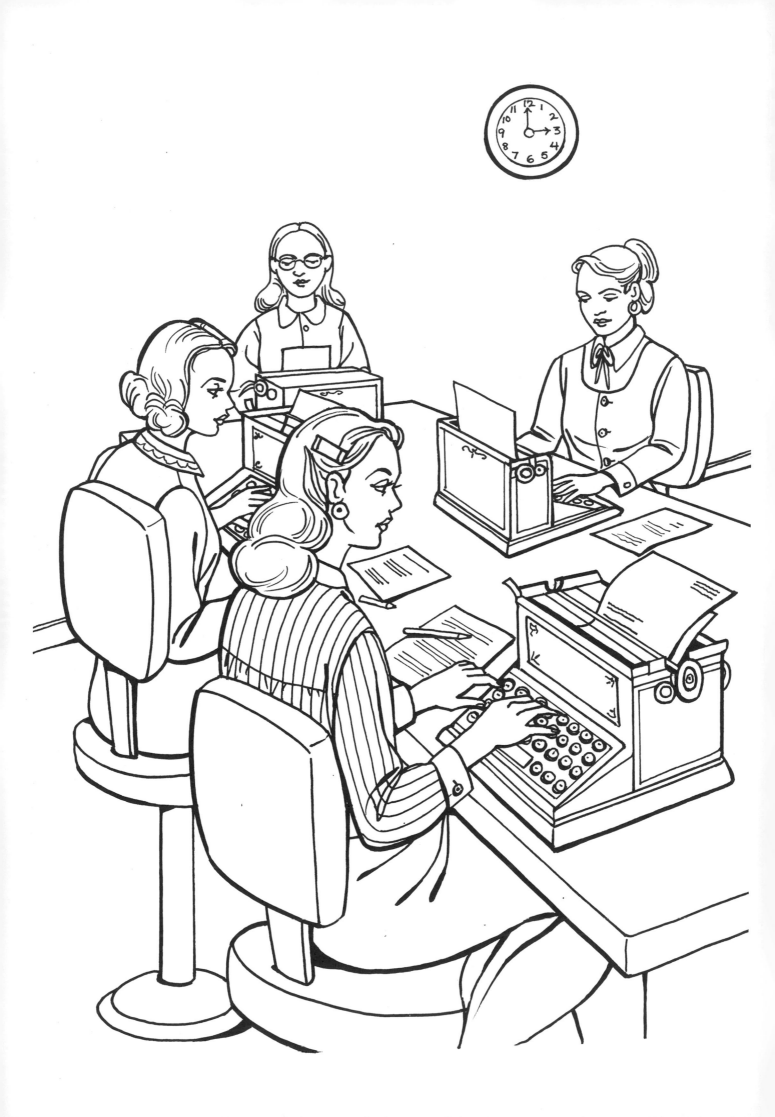

Go through your wardrobe

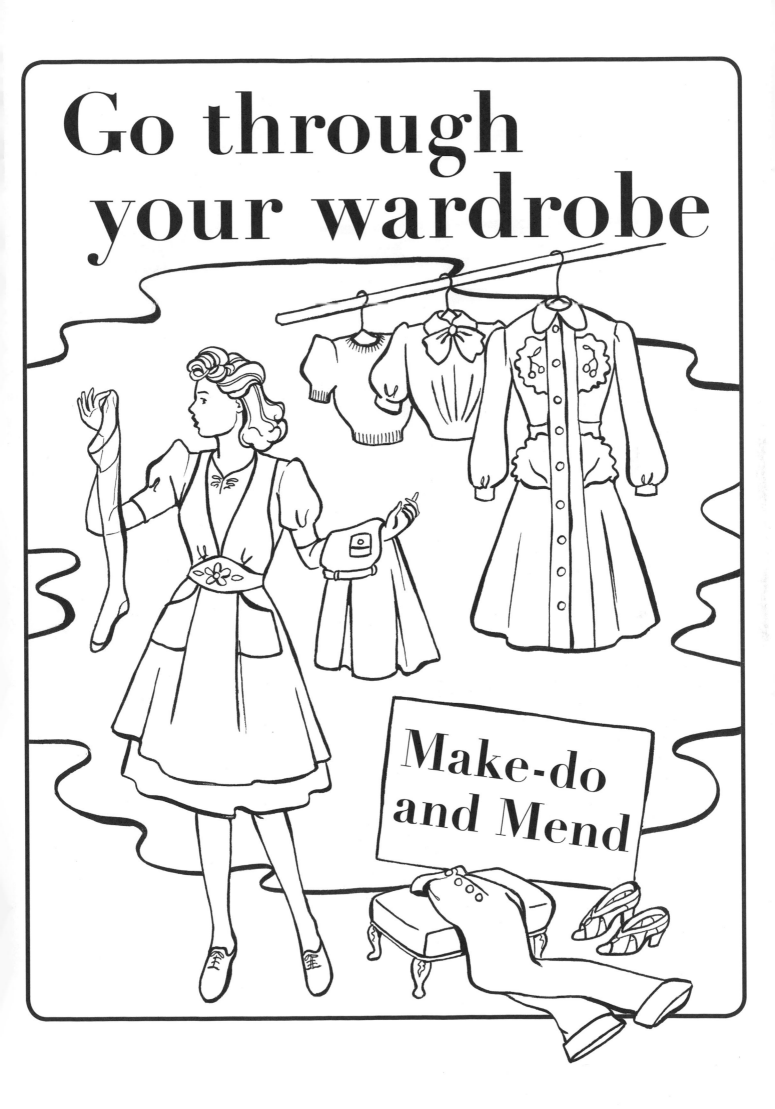

Make-do and Mend

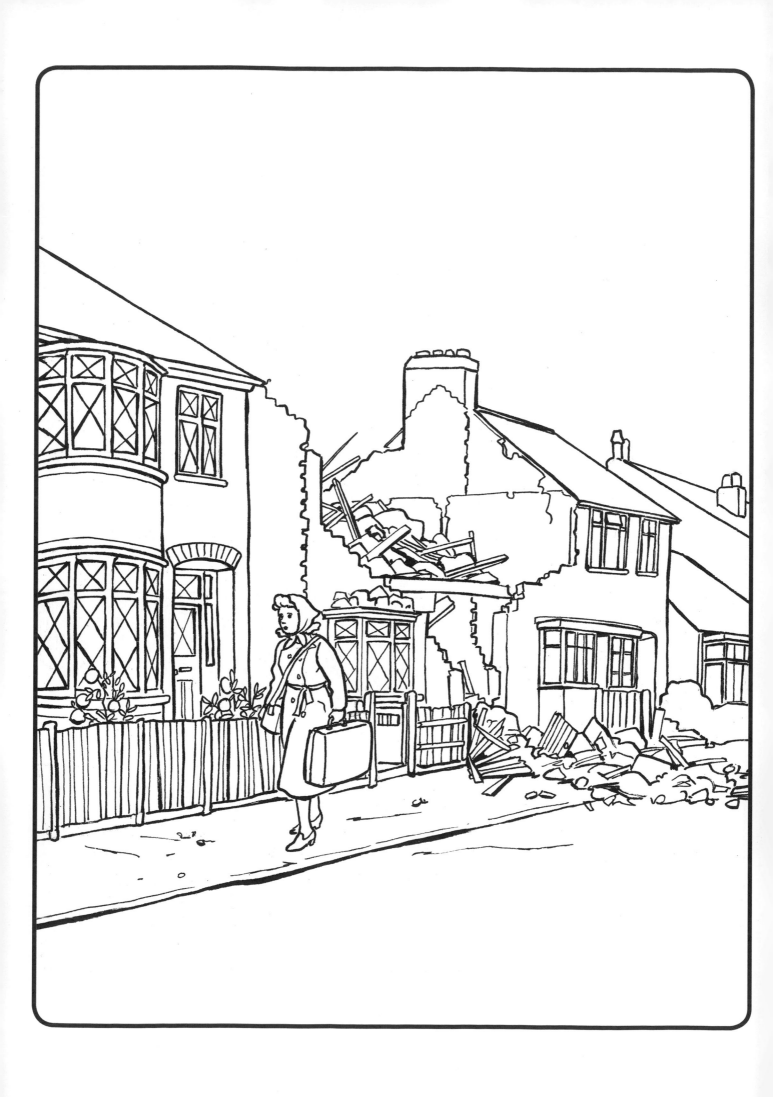

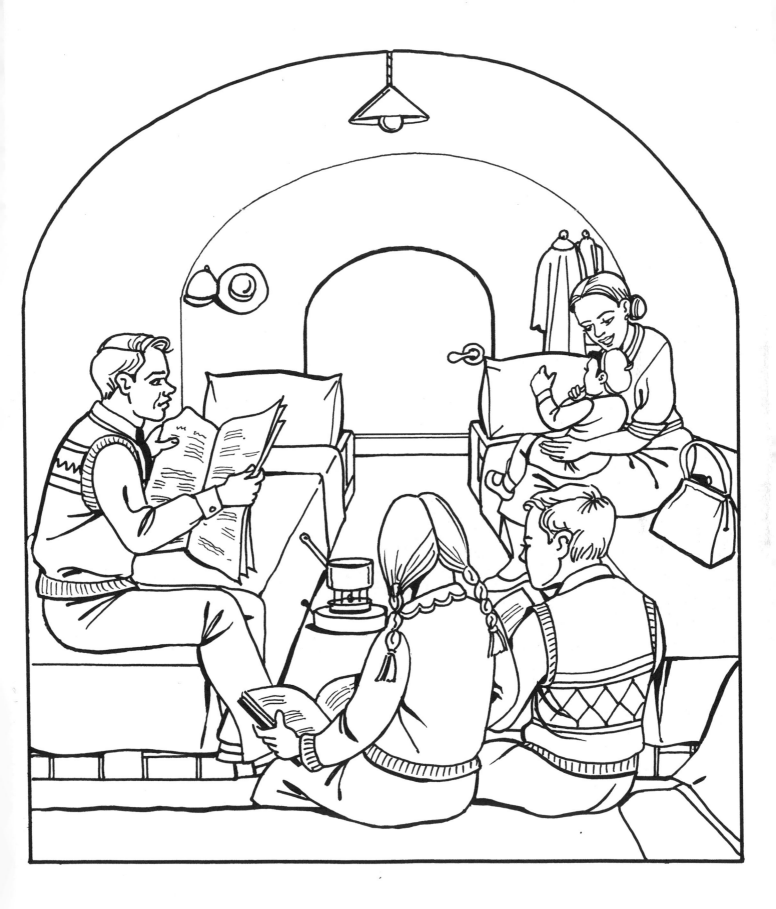

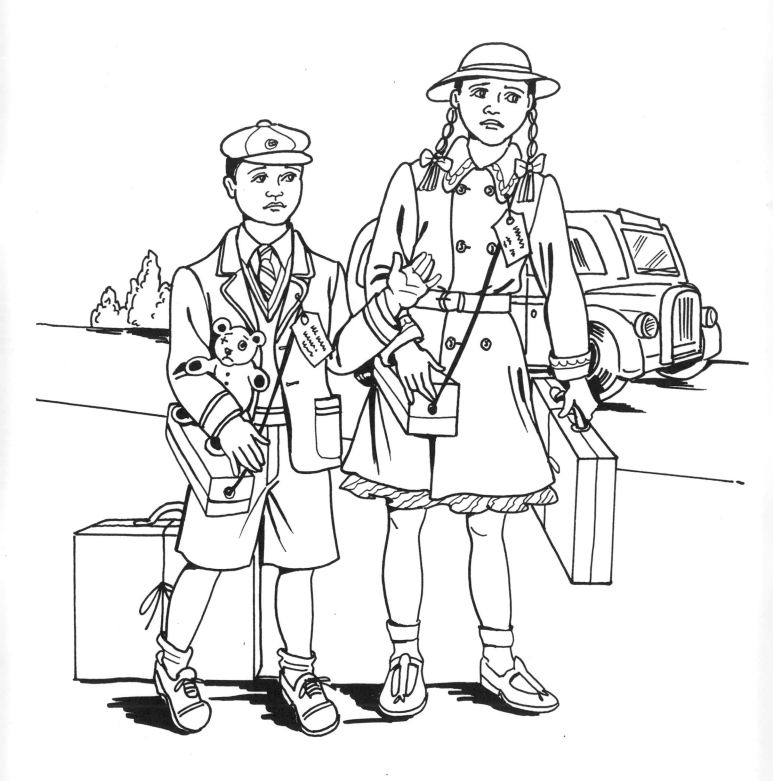

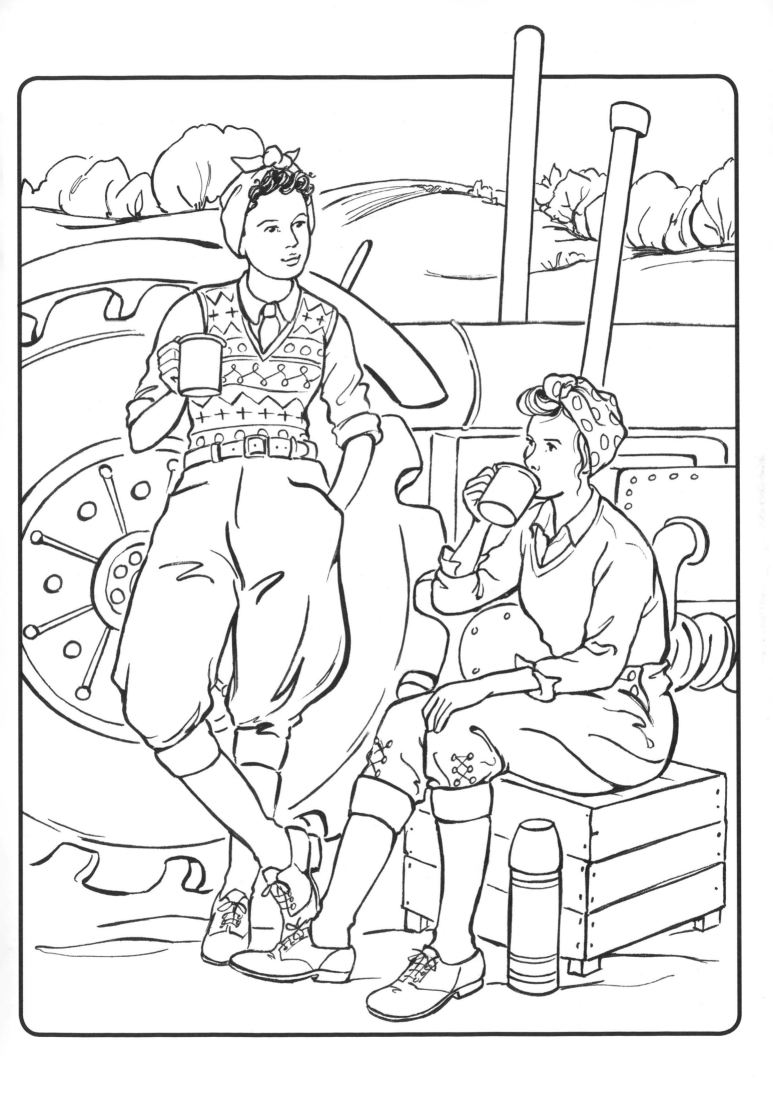

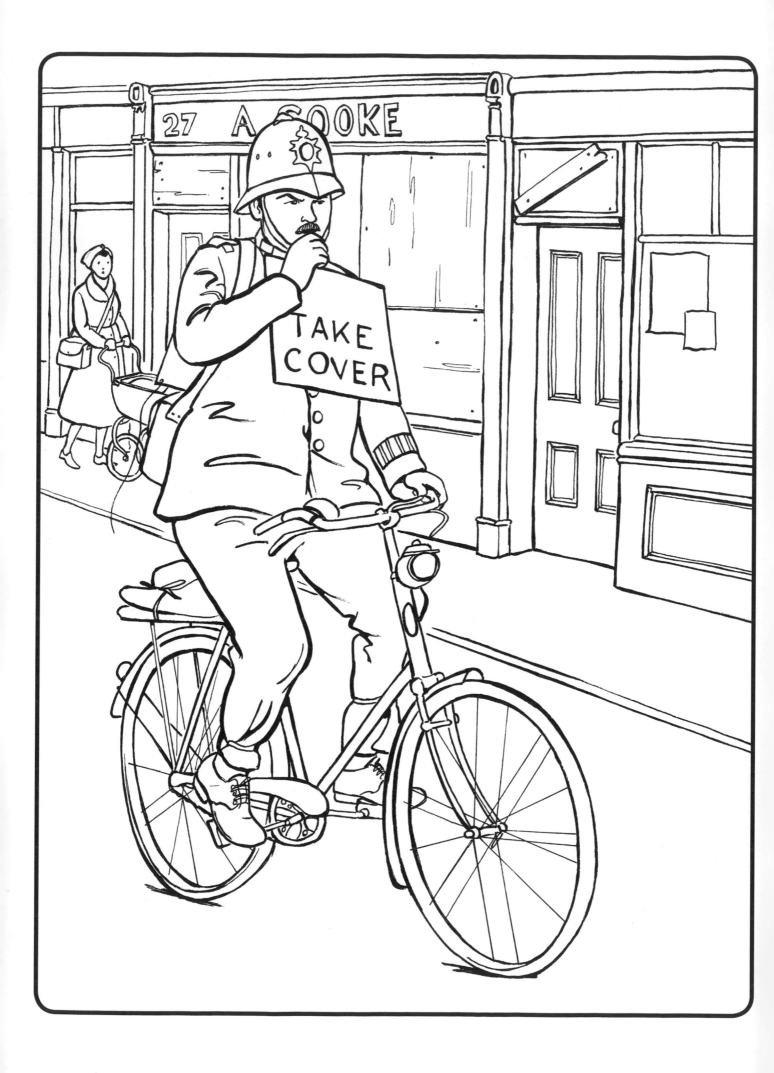

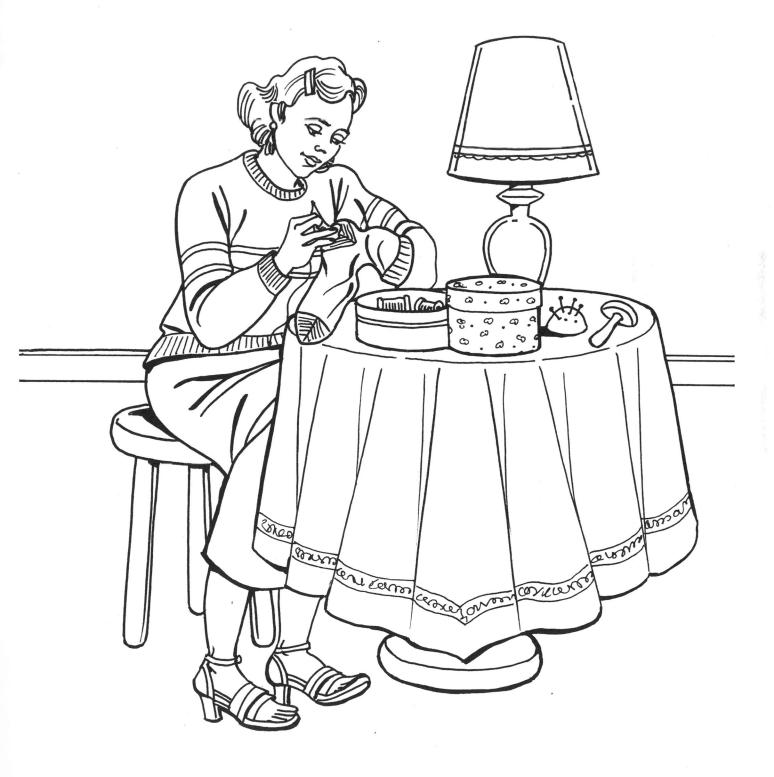

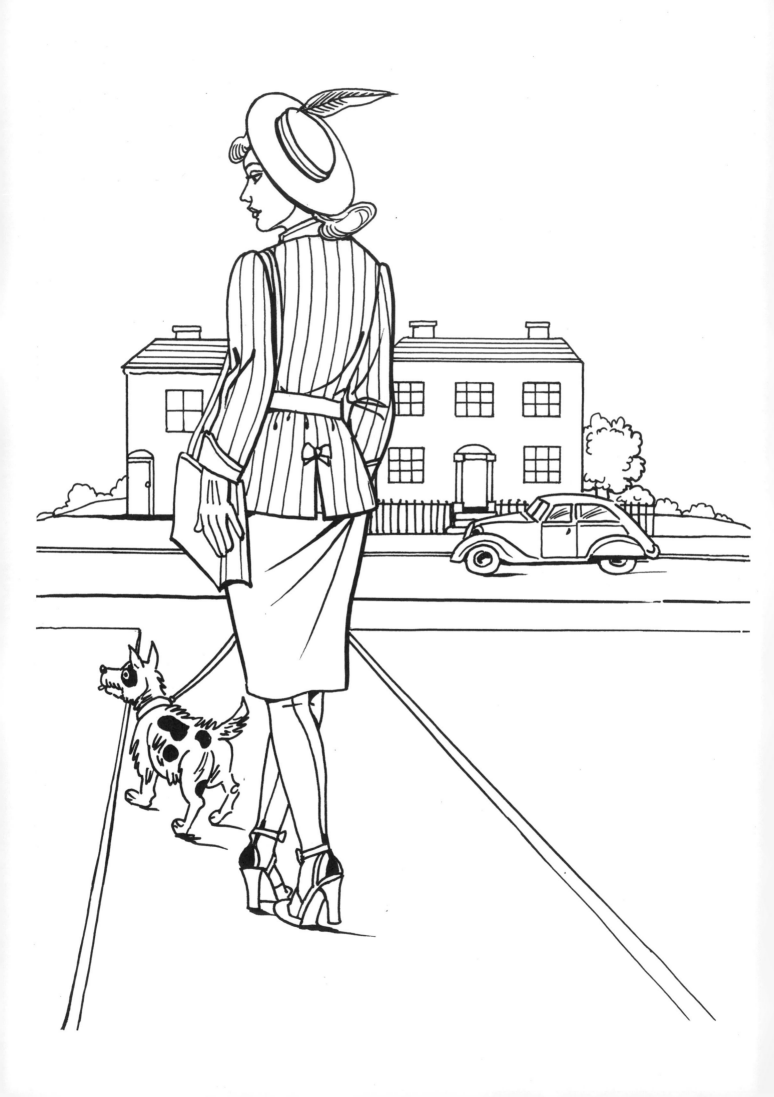

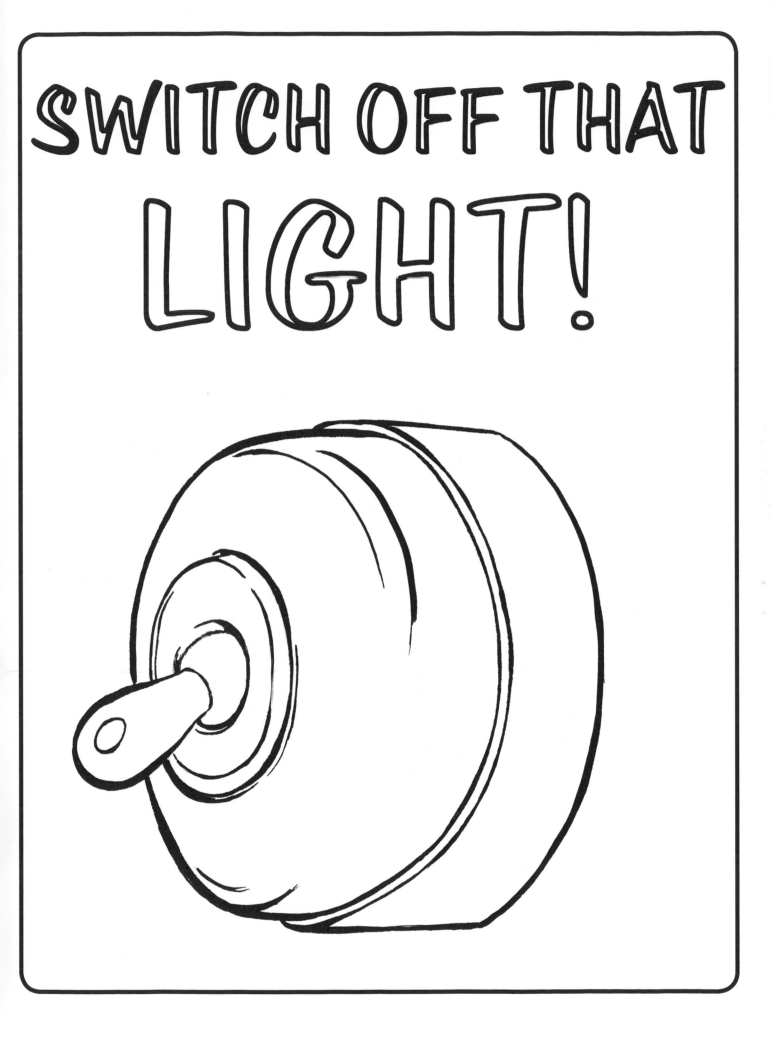

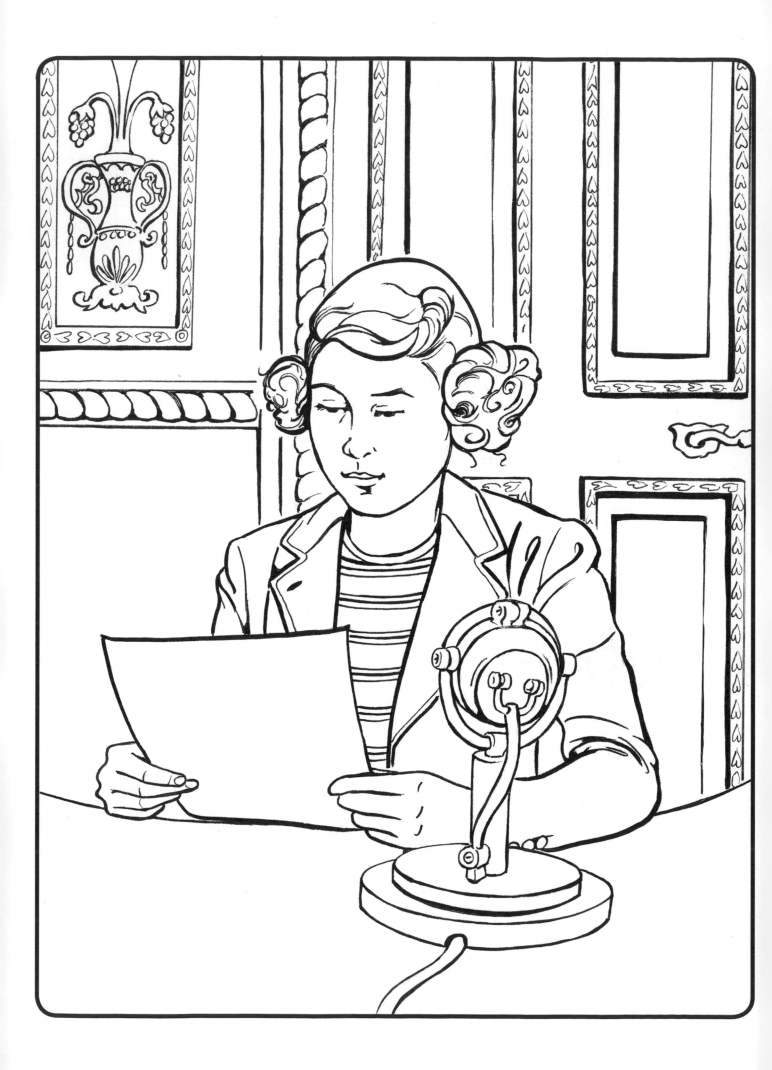

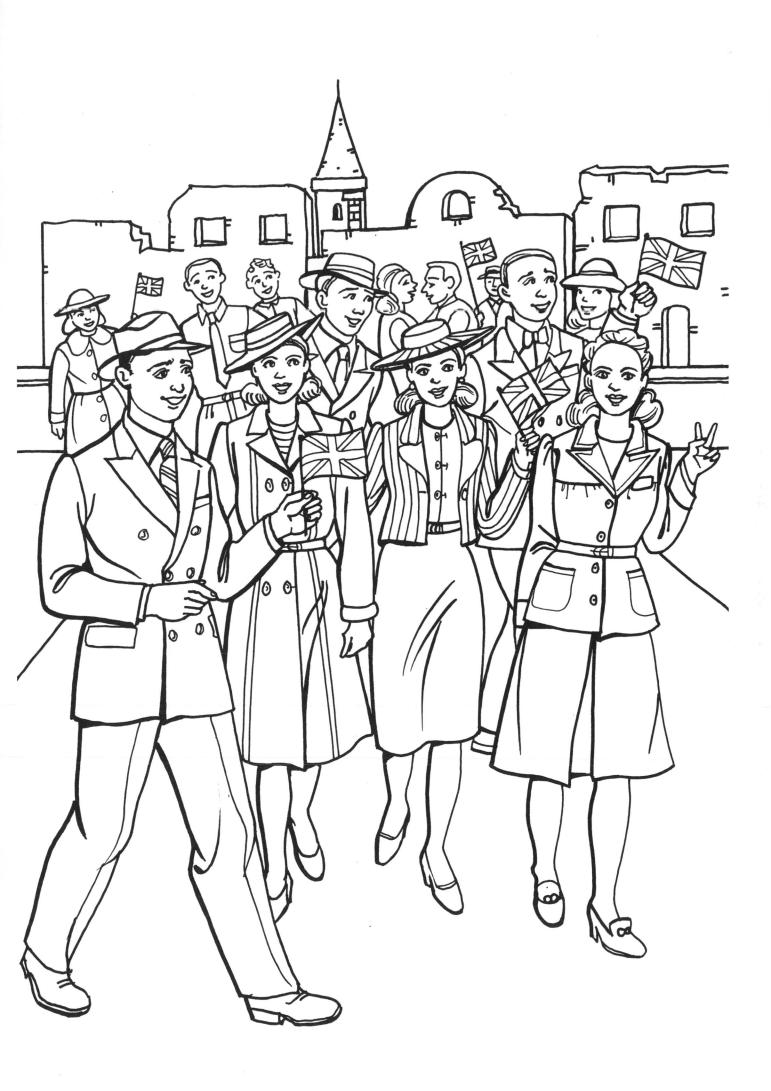

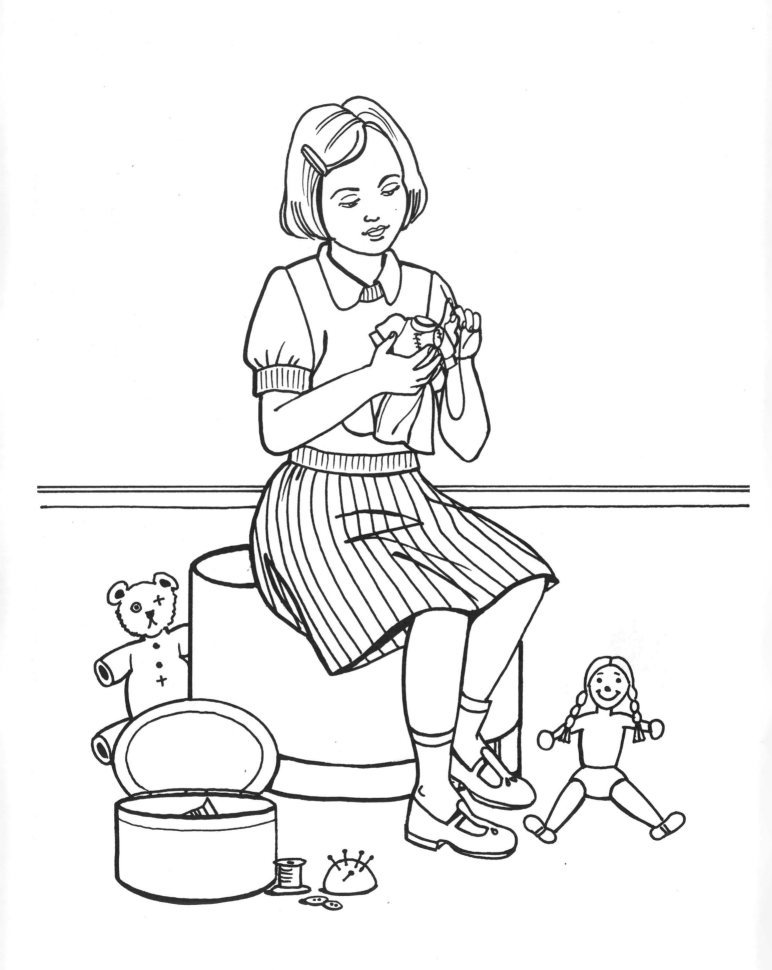

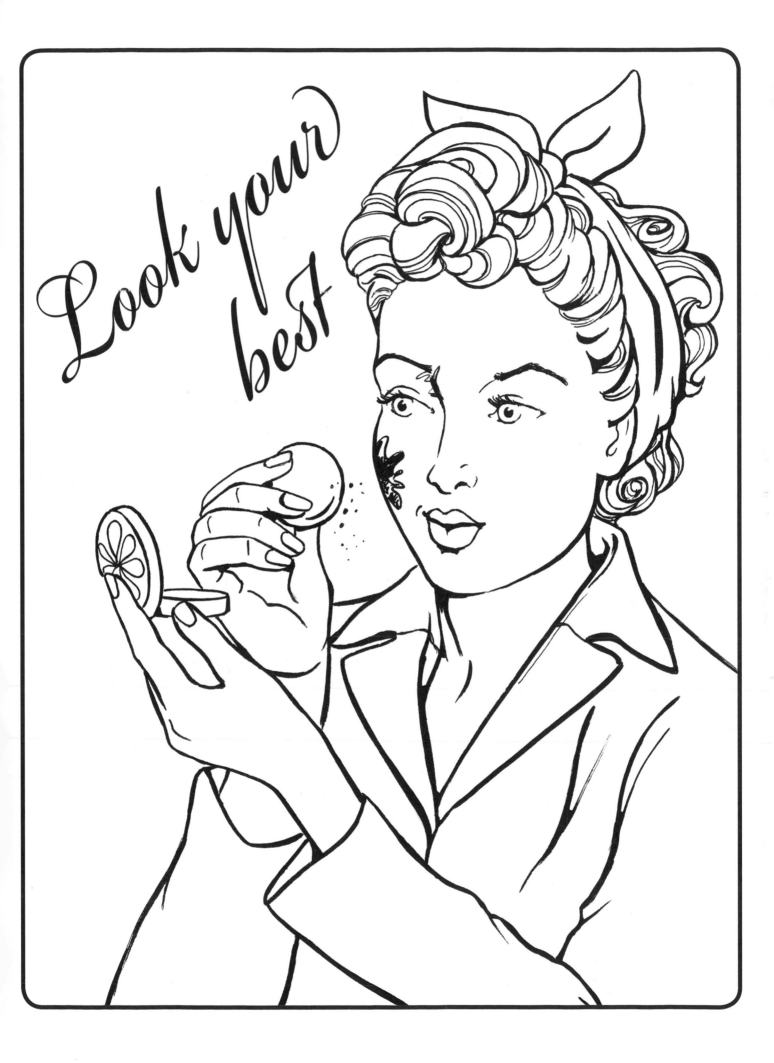

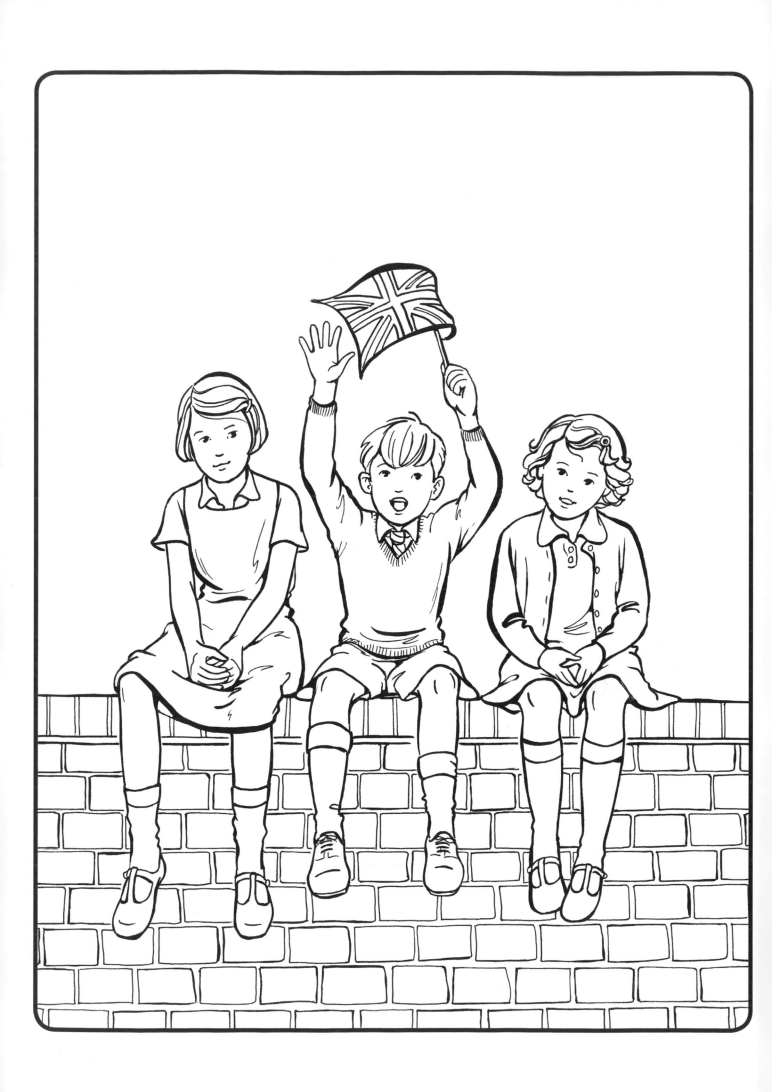

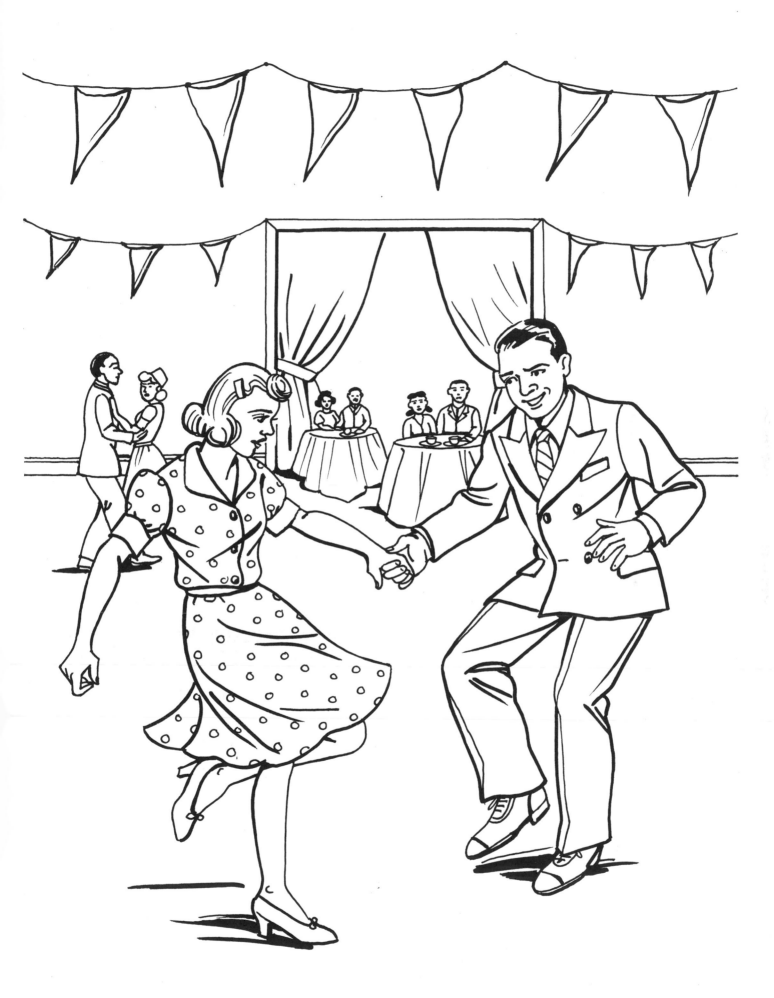

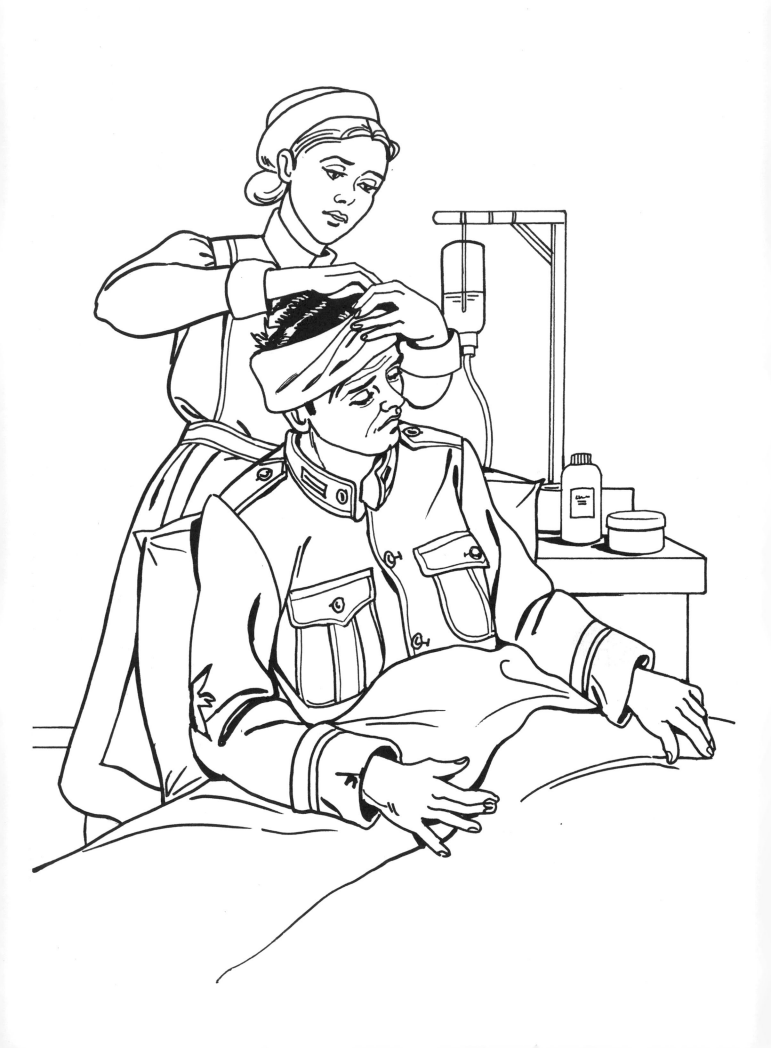

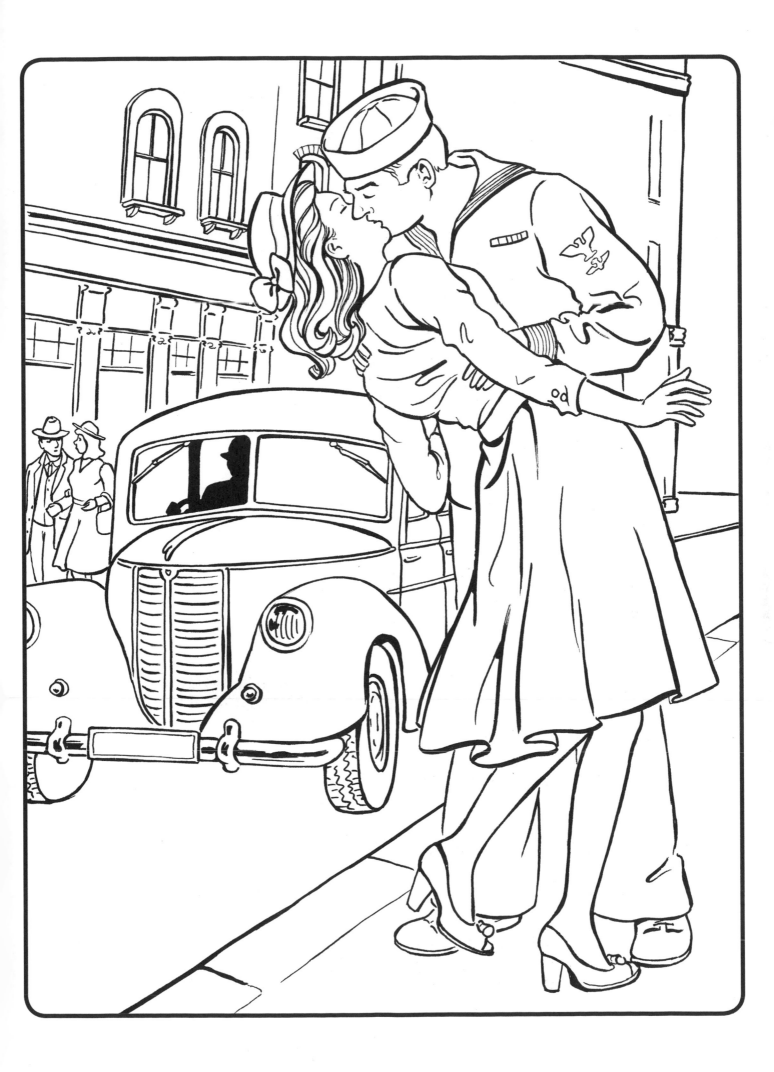

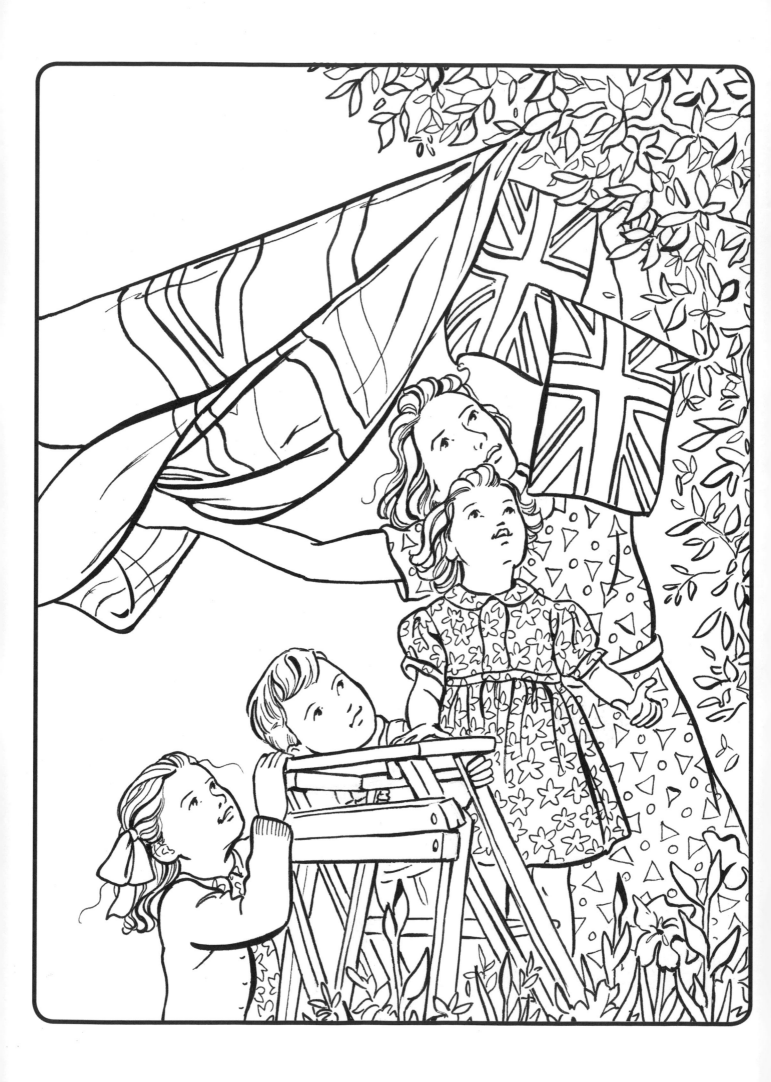

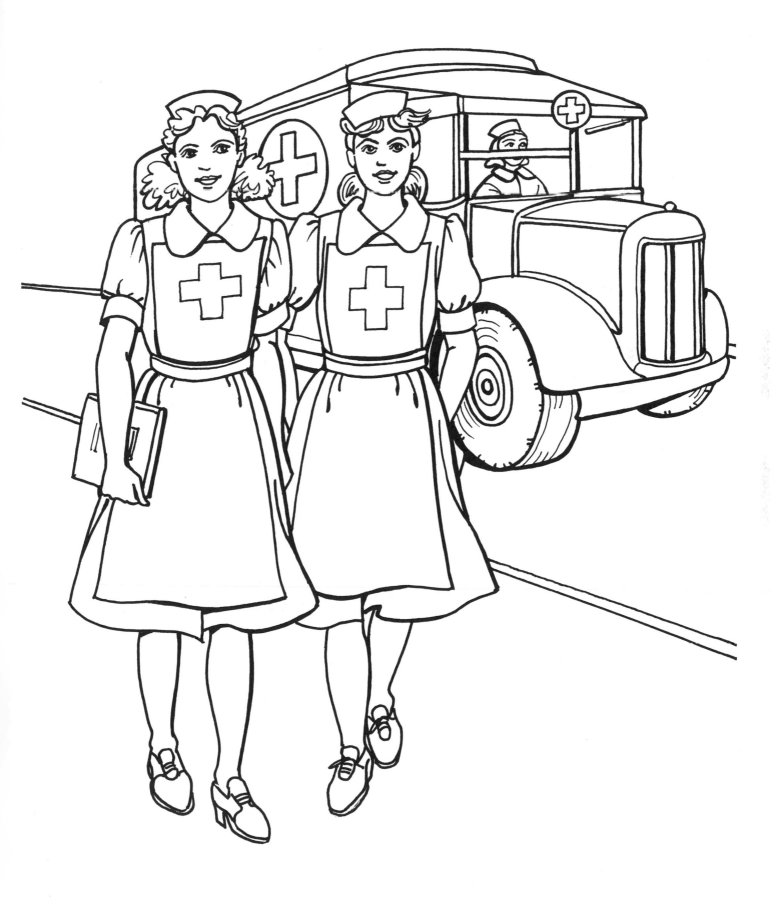

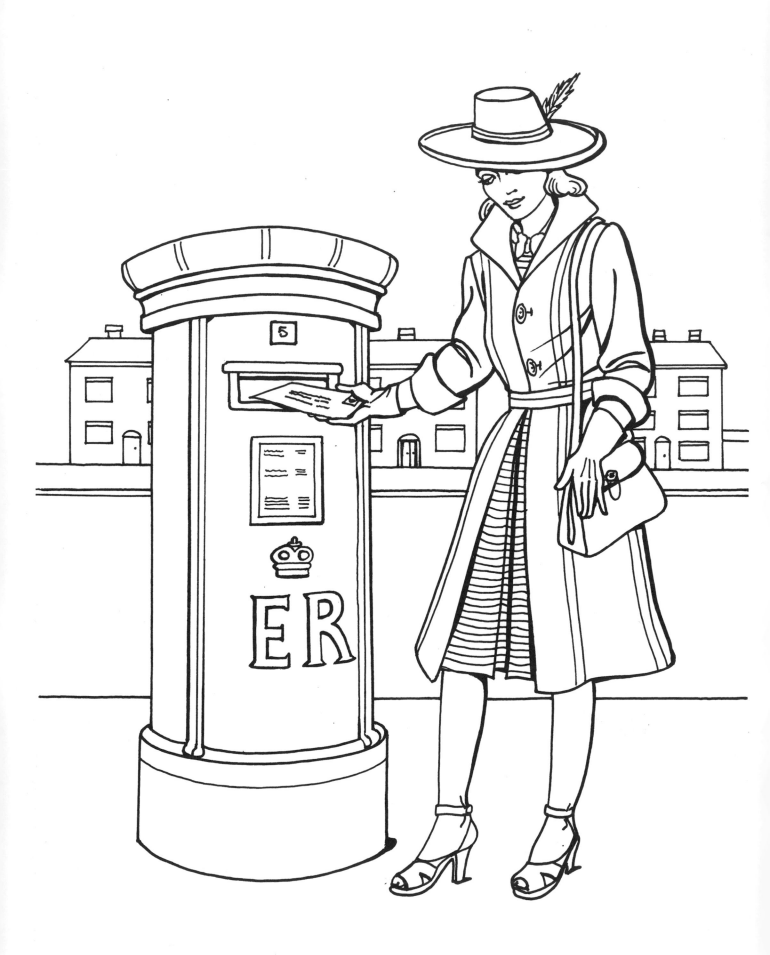

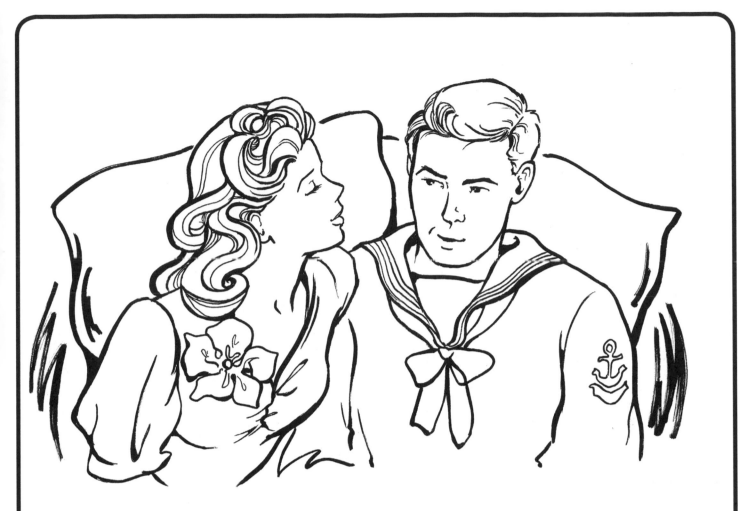

CARELESS TALK
COSTS LIVES!
TELL NOBODY - NOT EVEN HER!

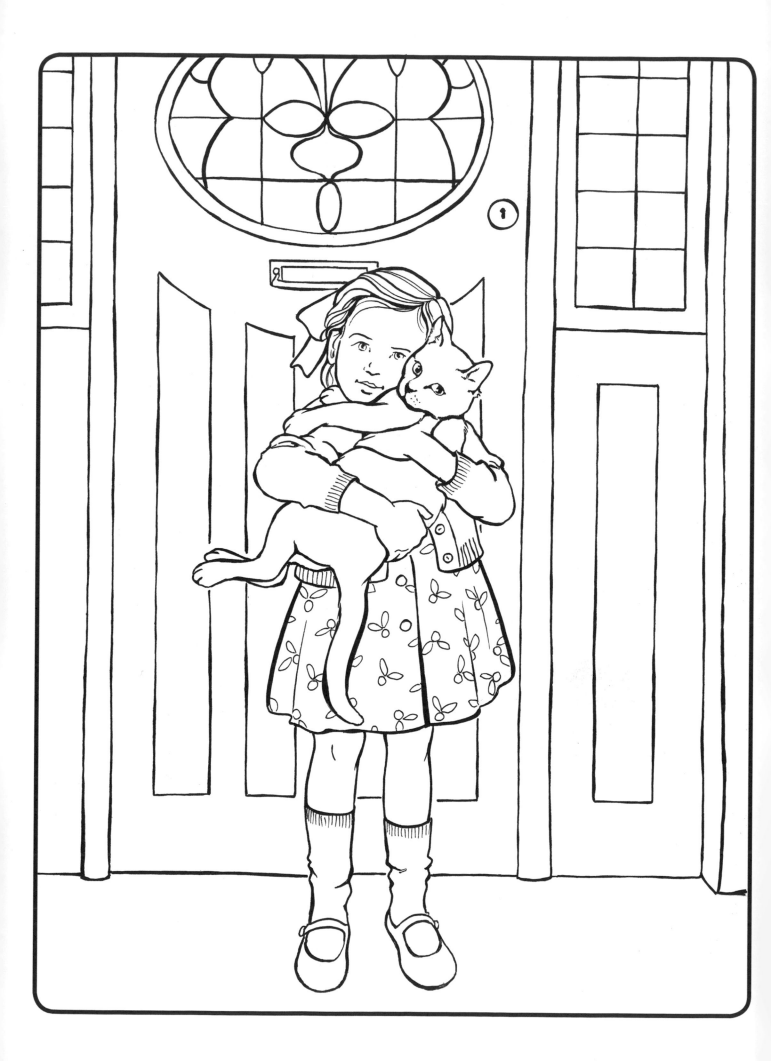

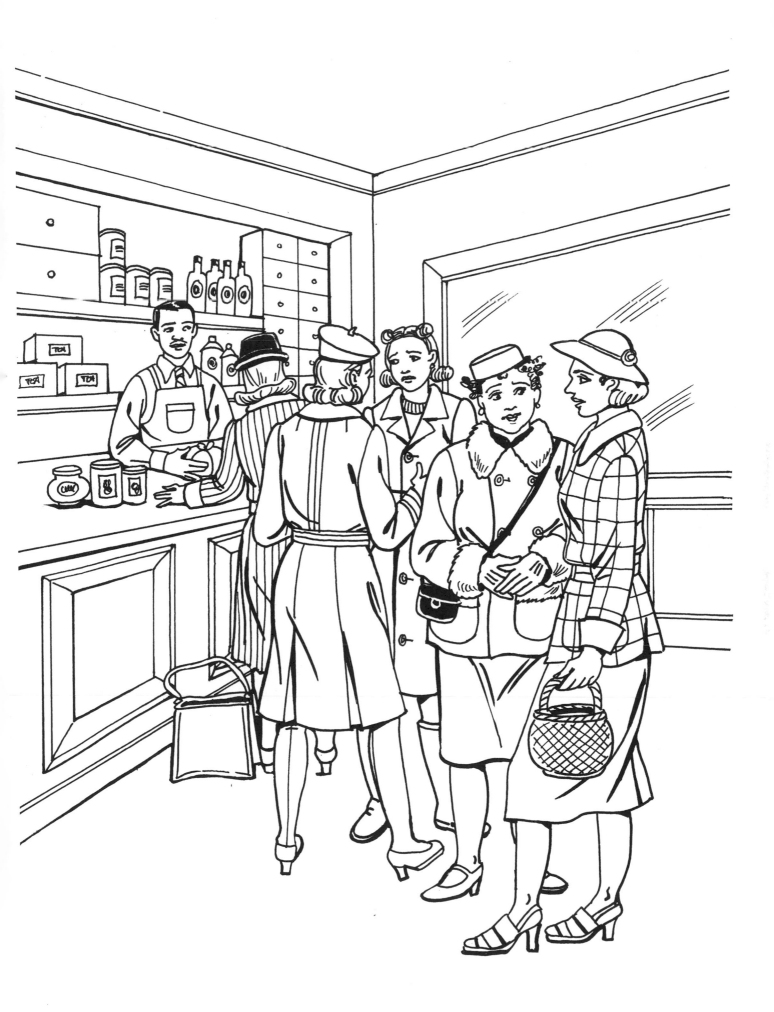

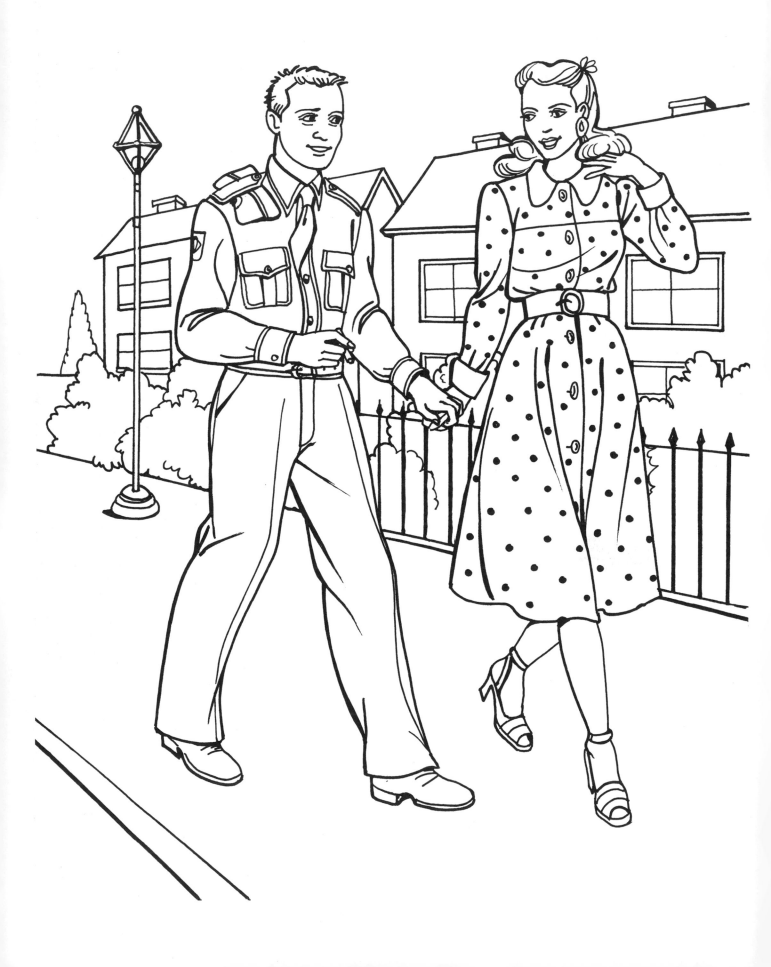

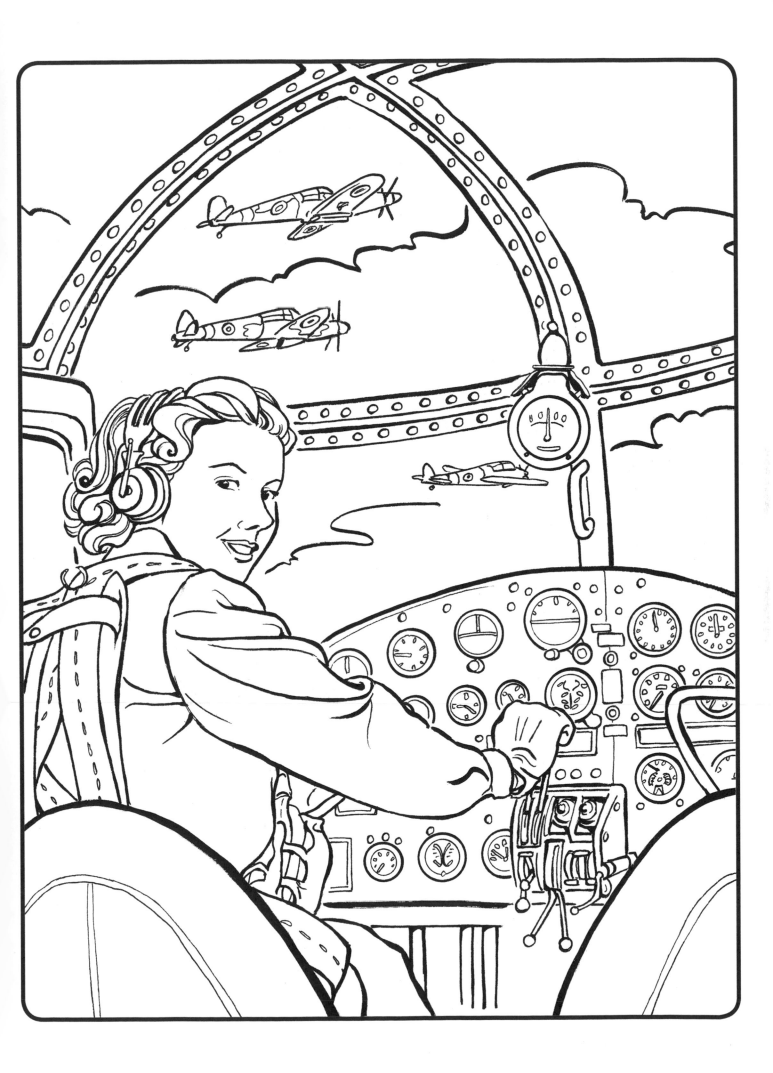

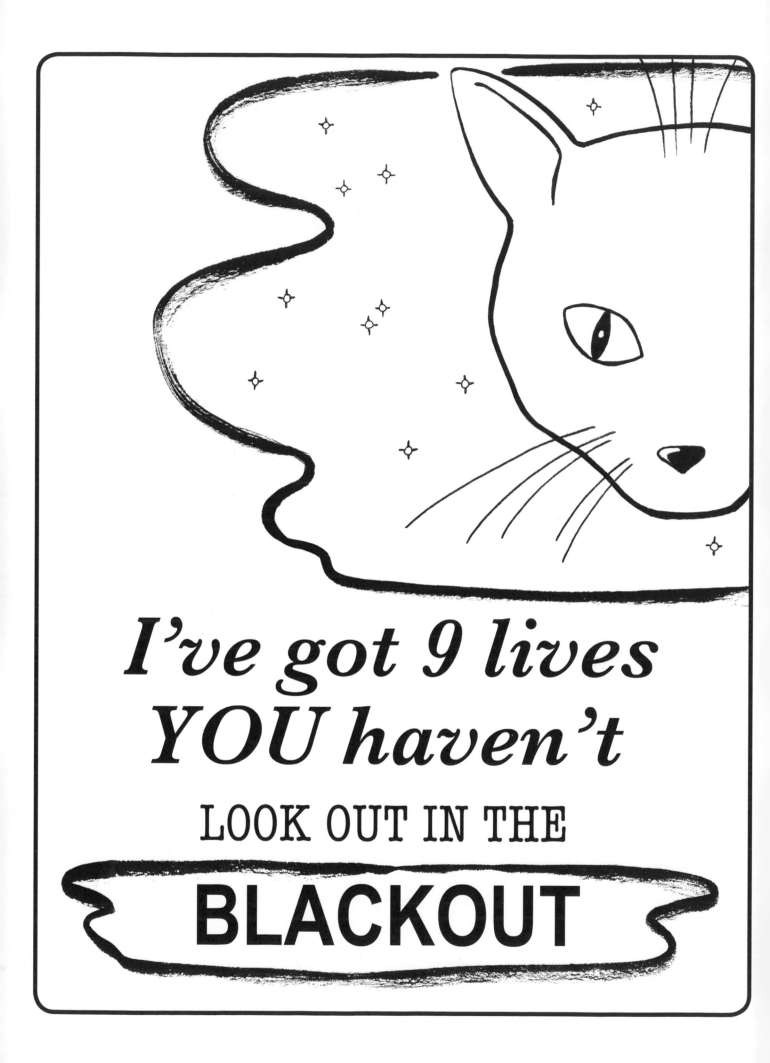

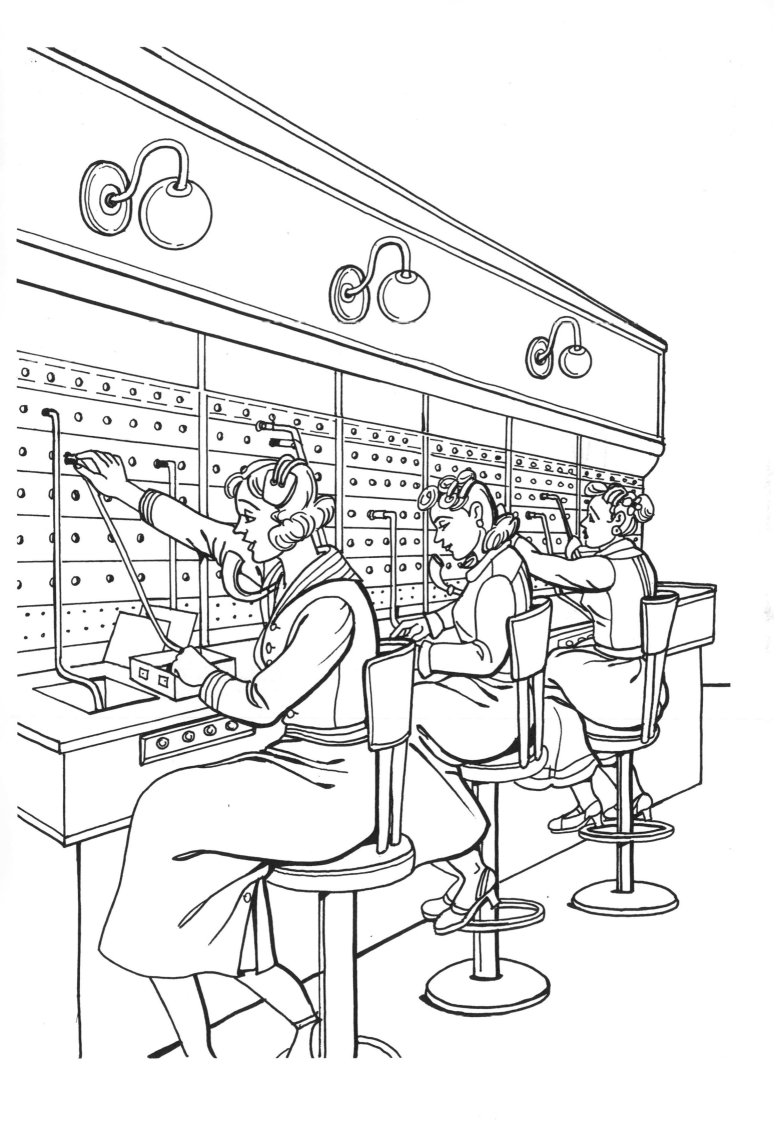

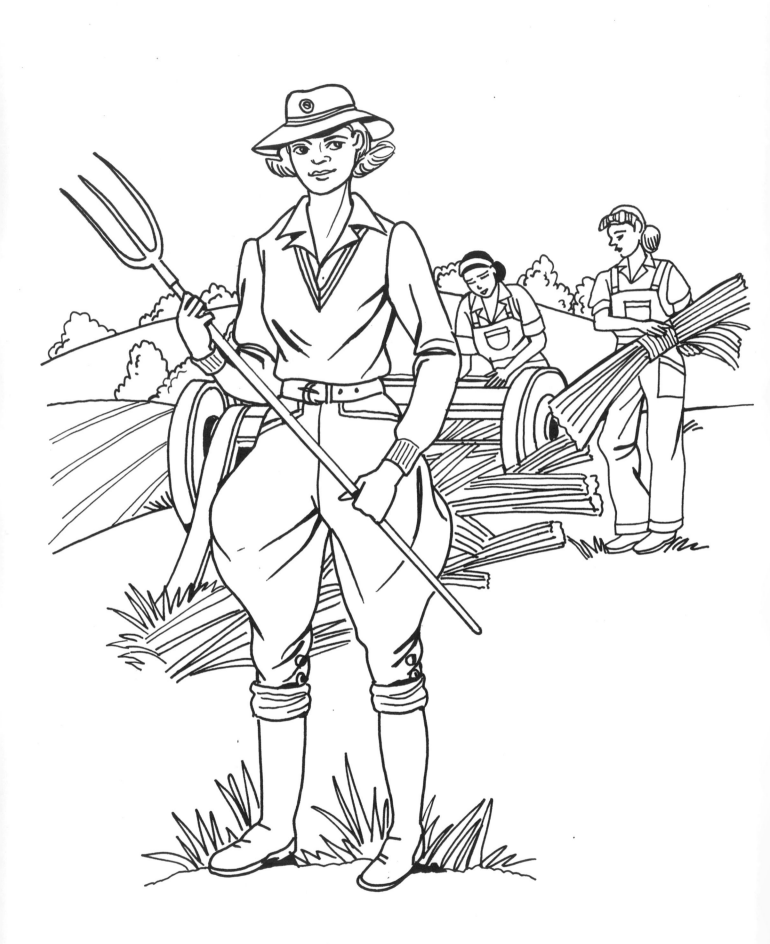

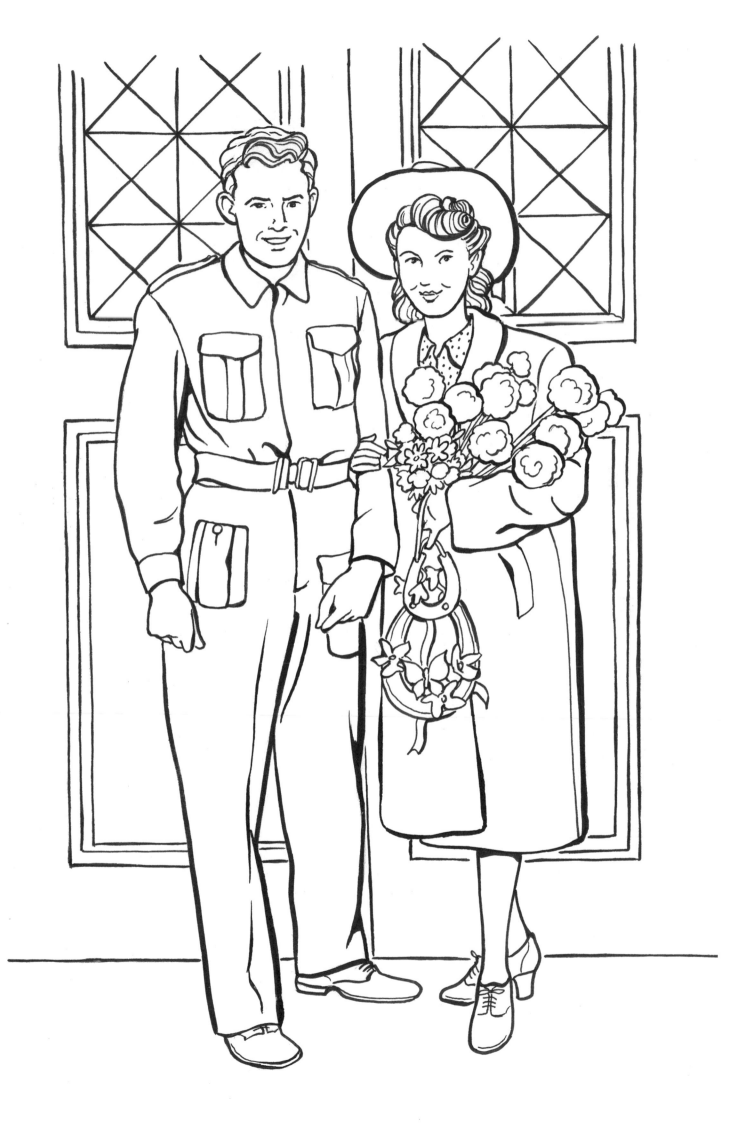

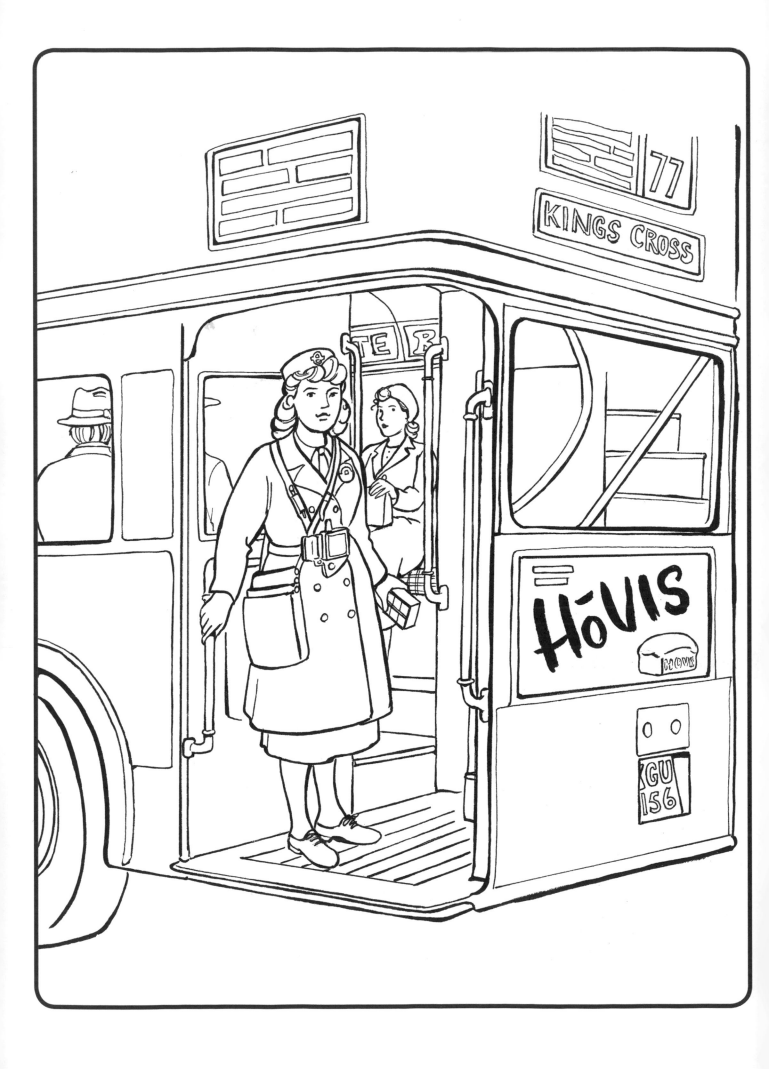

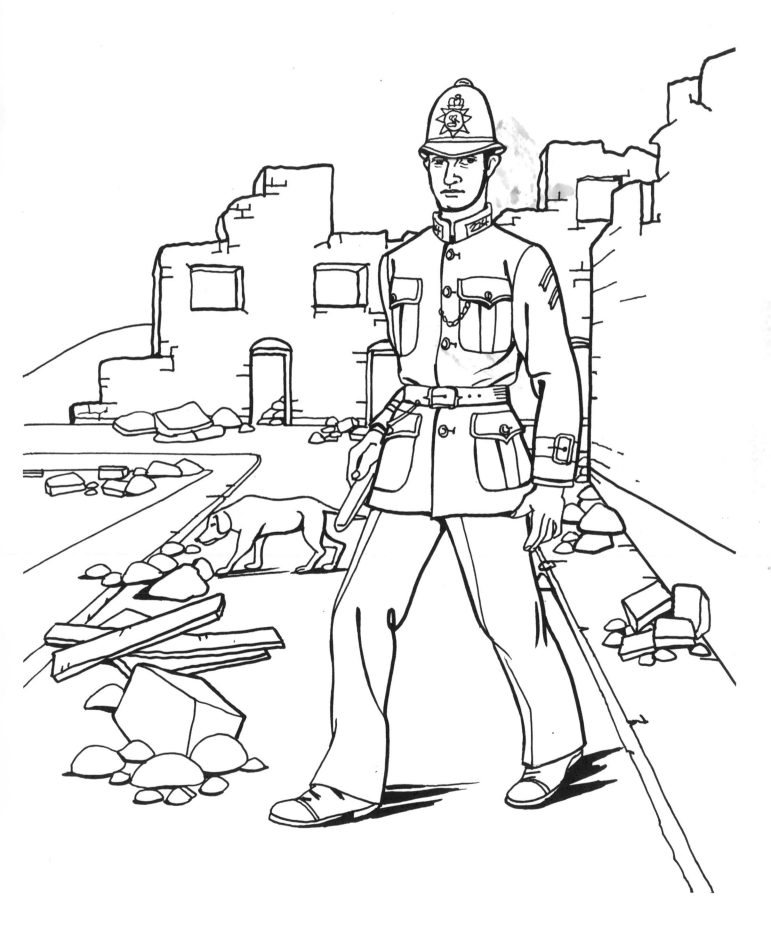

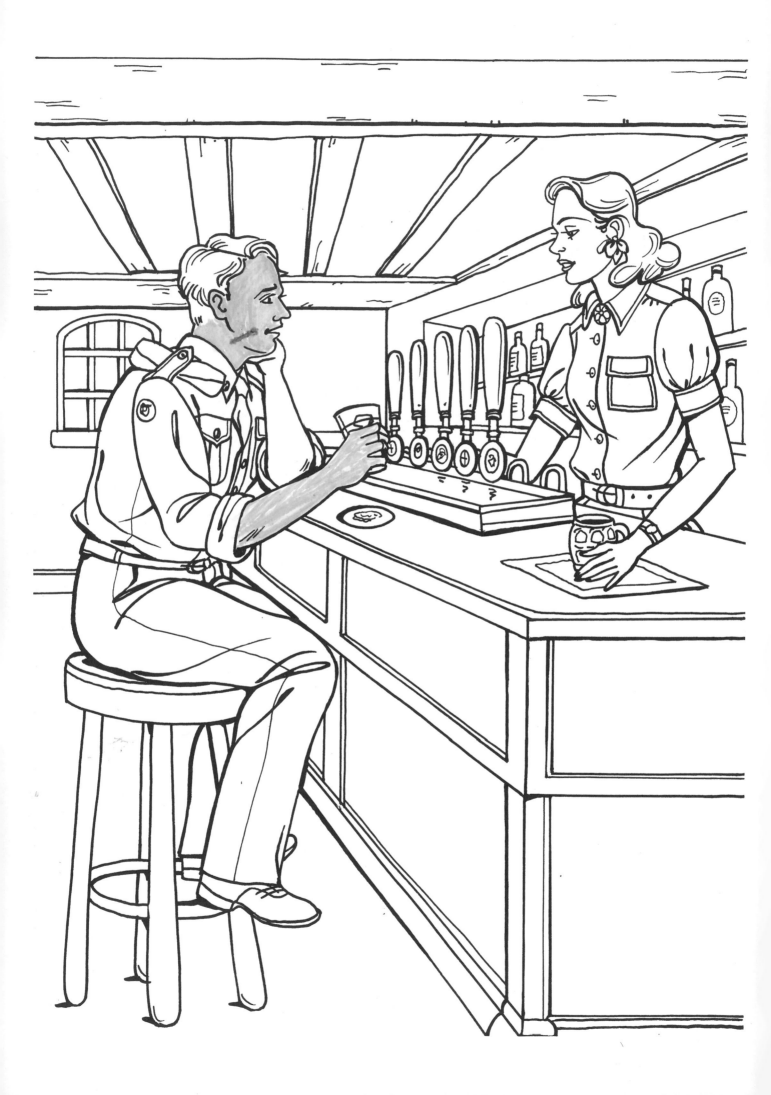

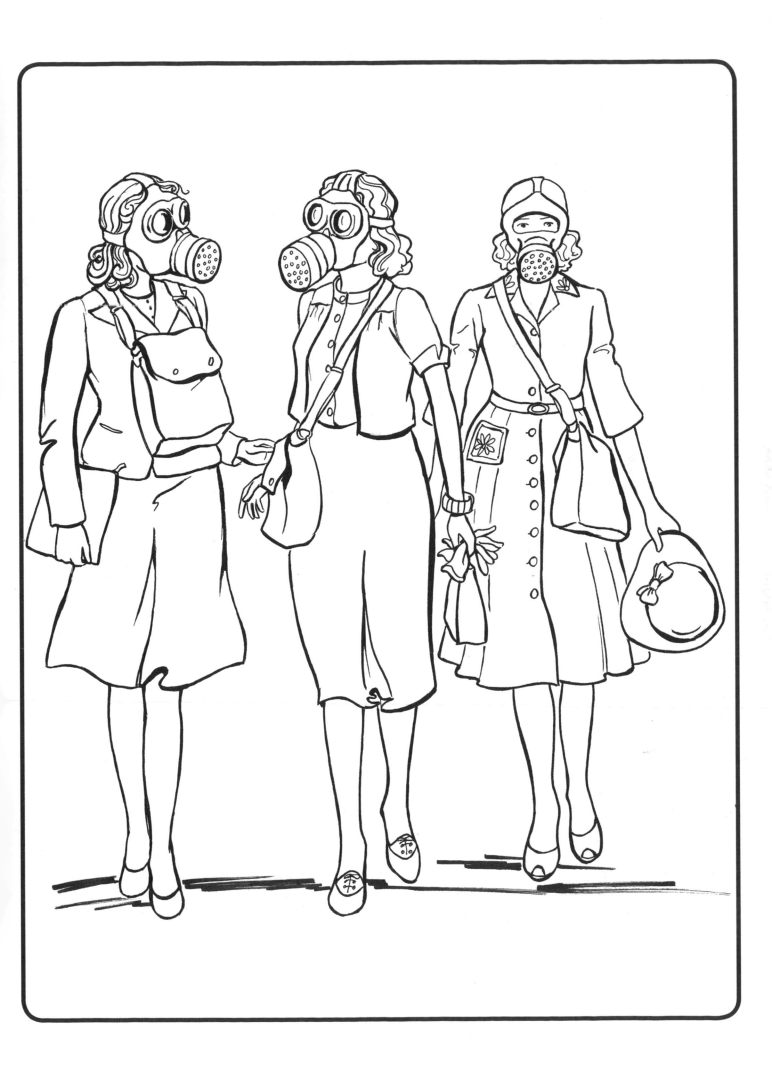

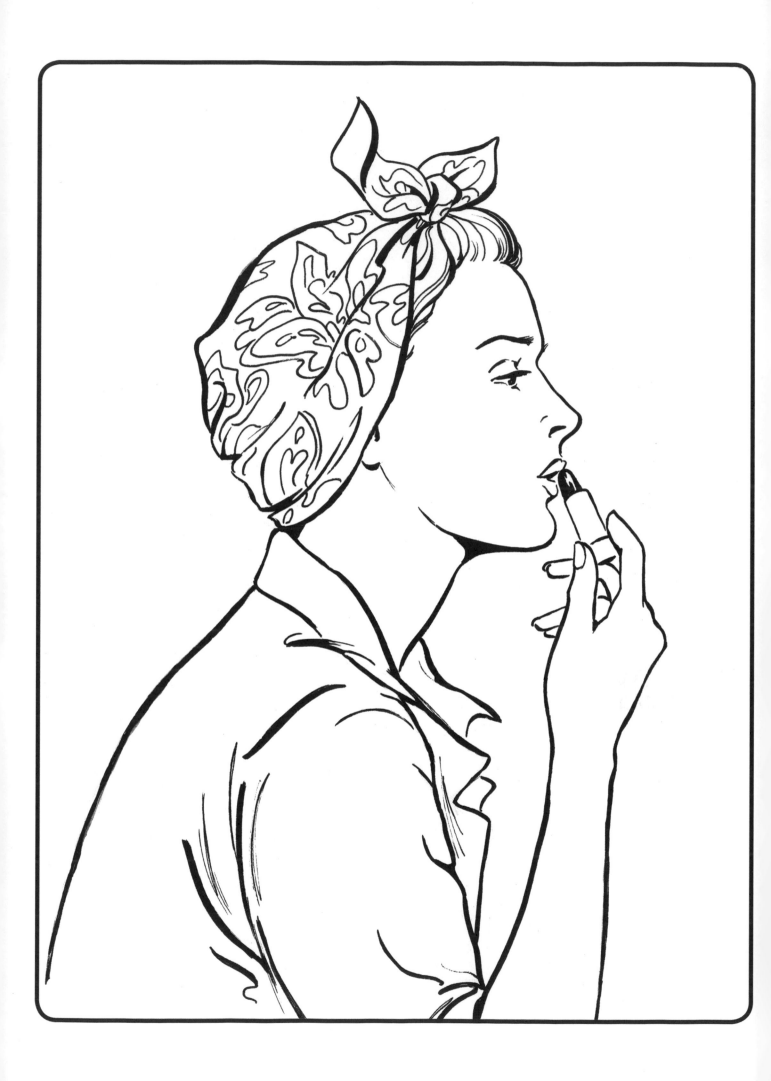

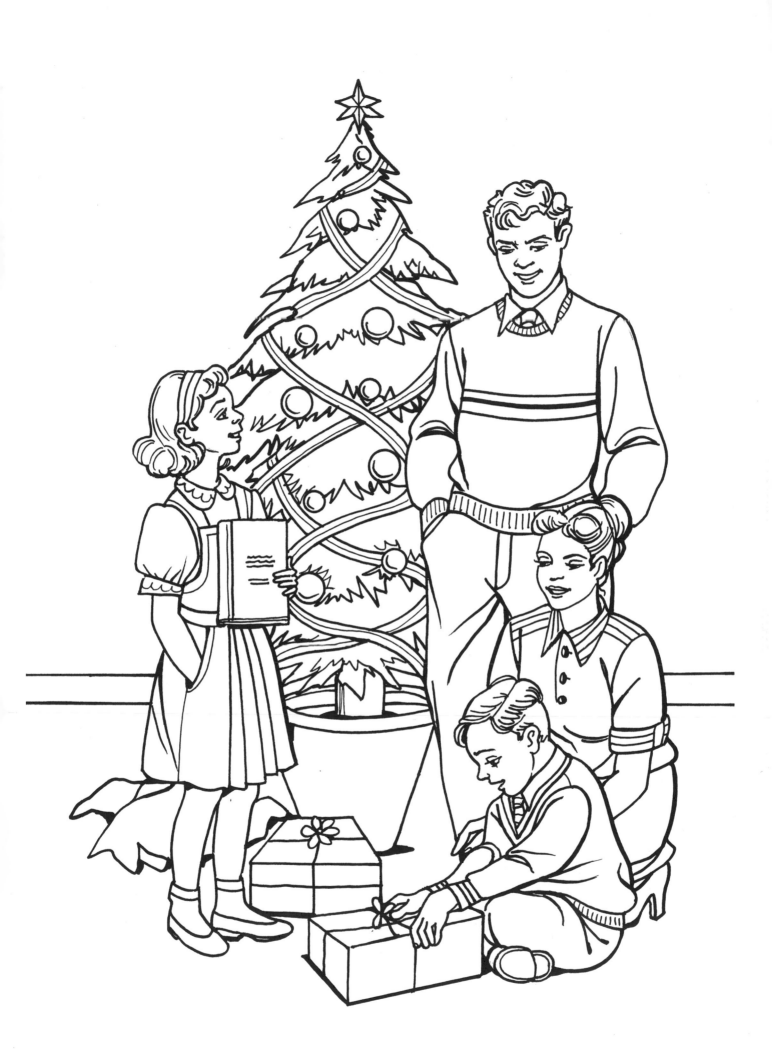

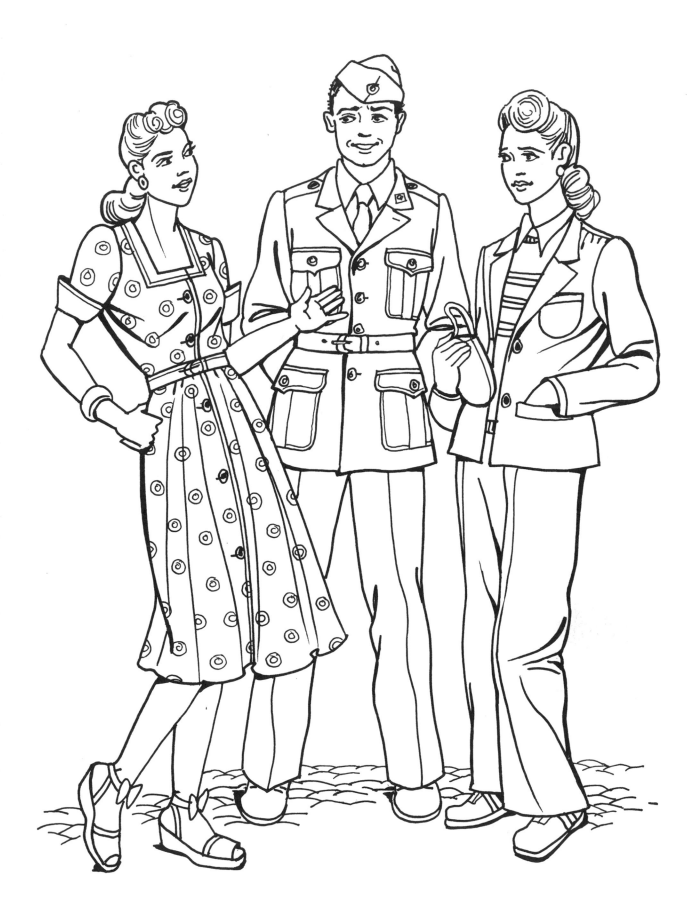

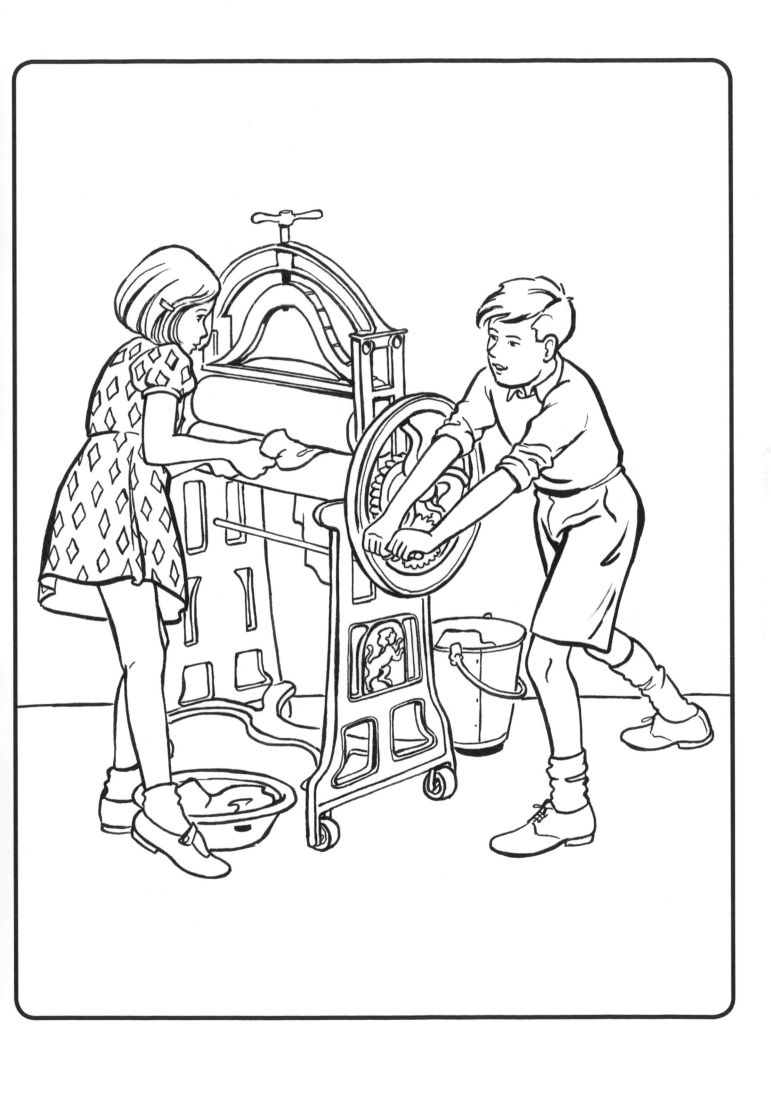

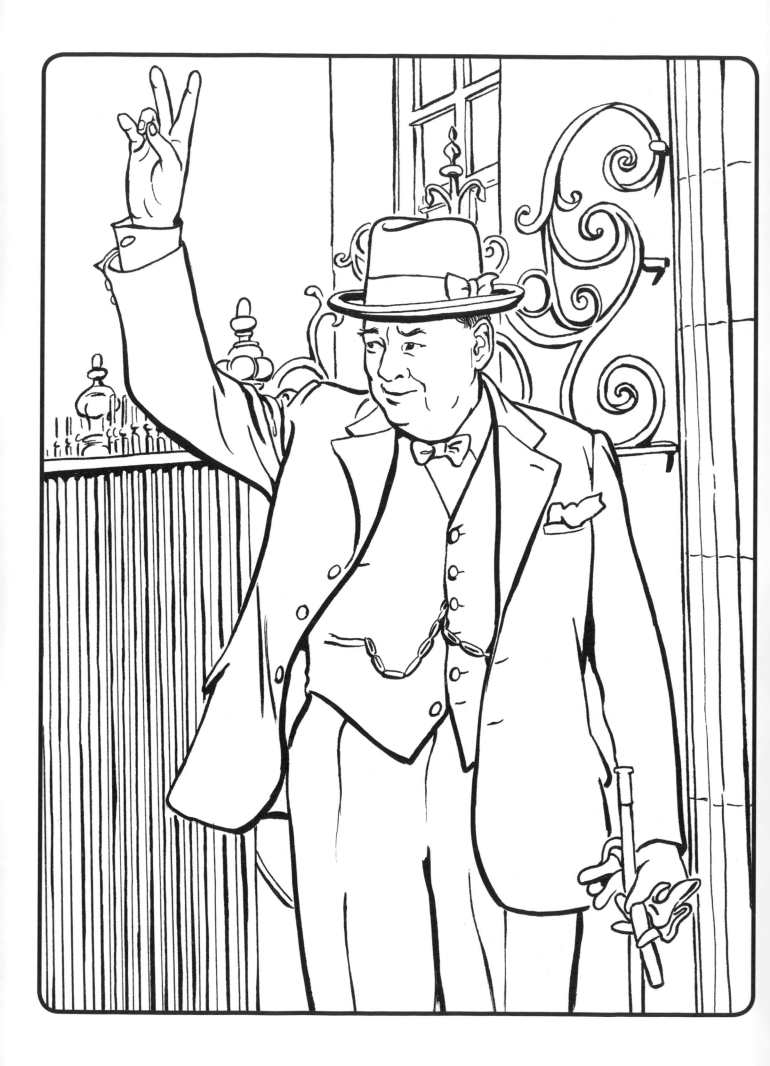

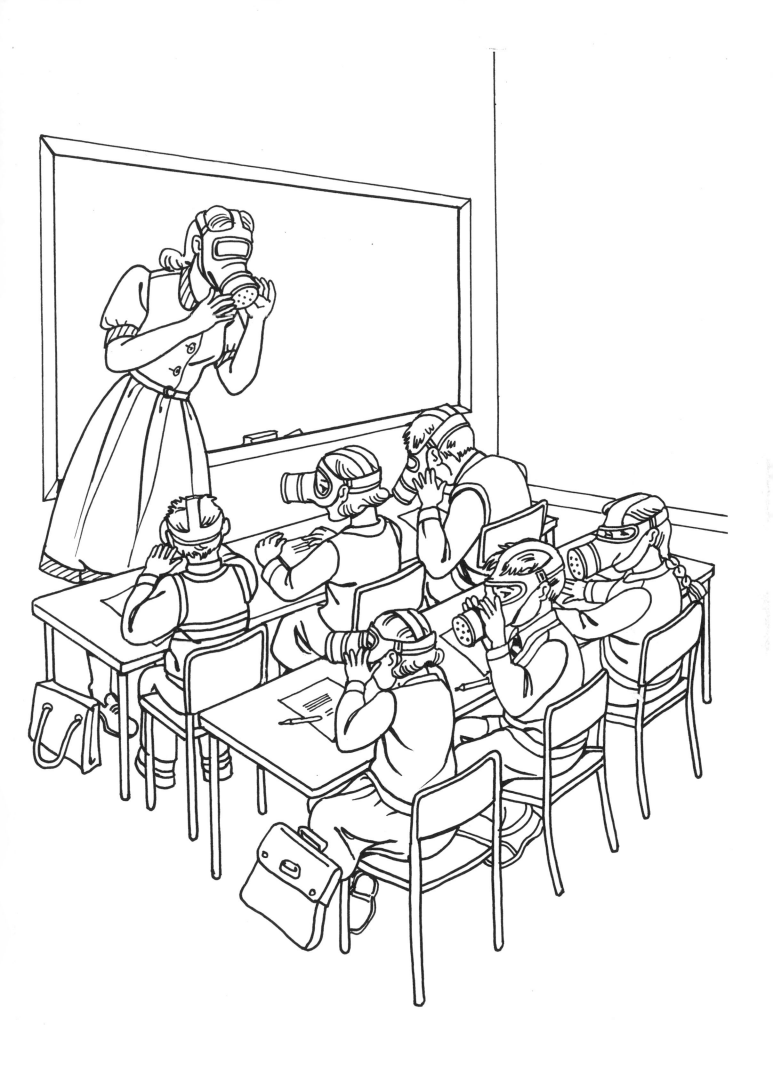

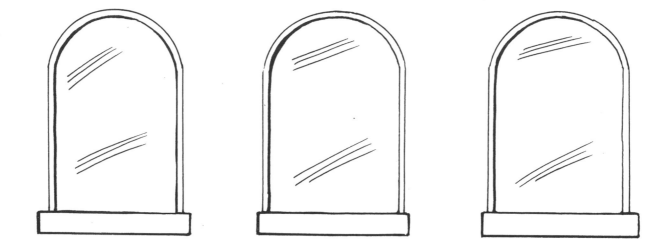
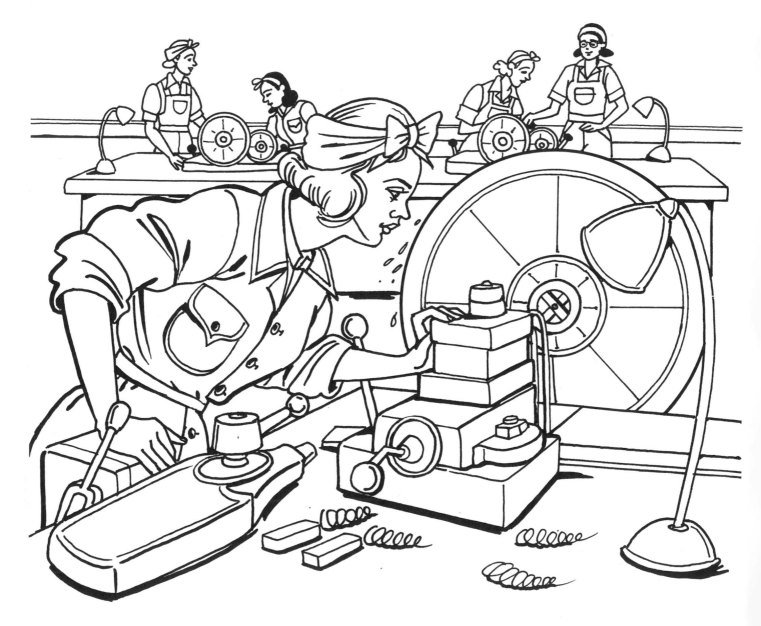

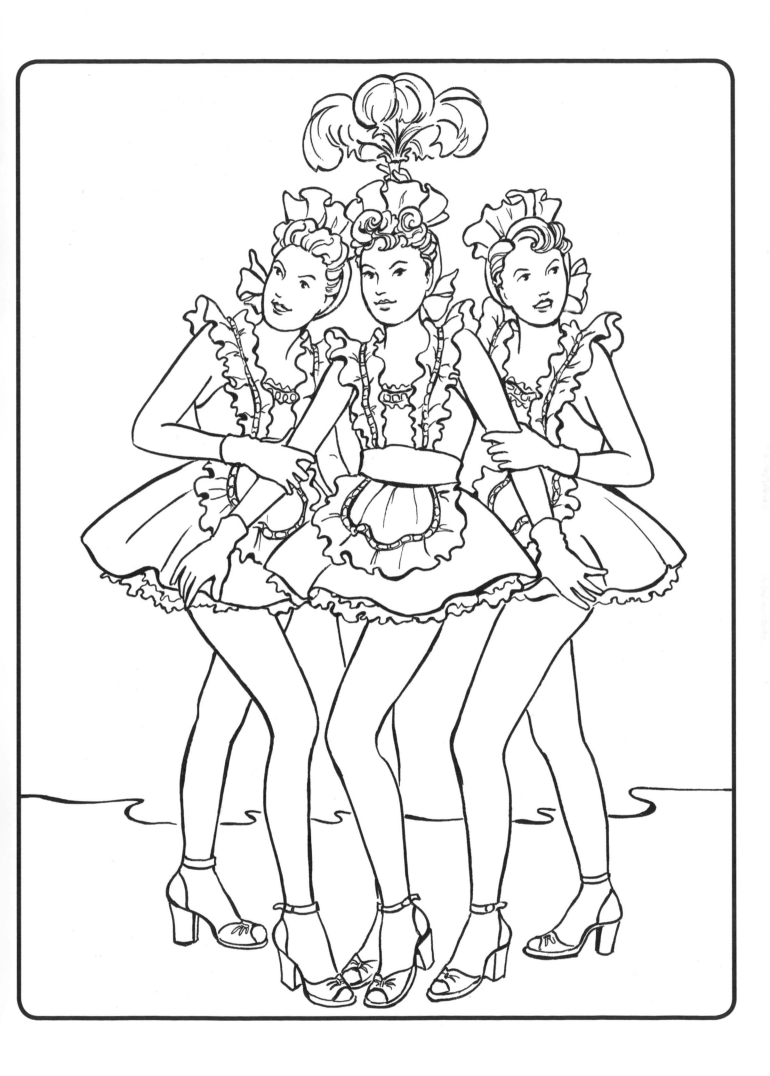

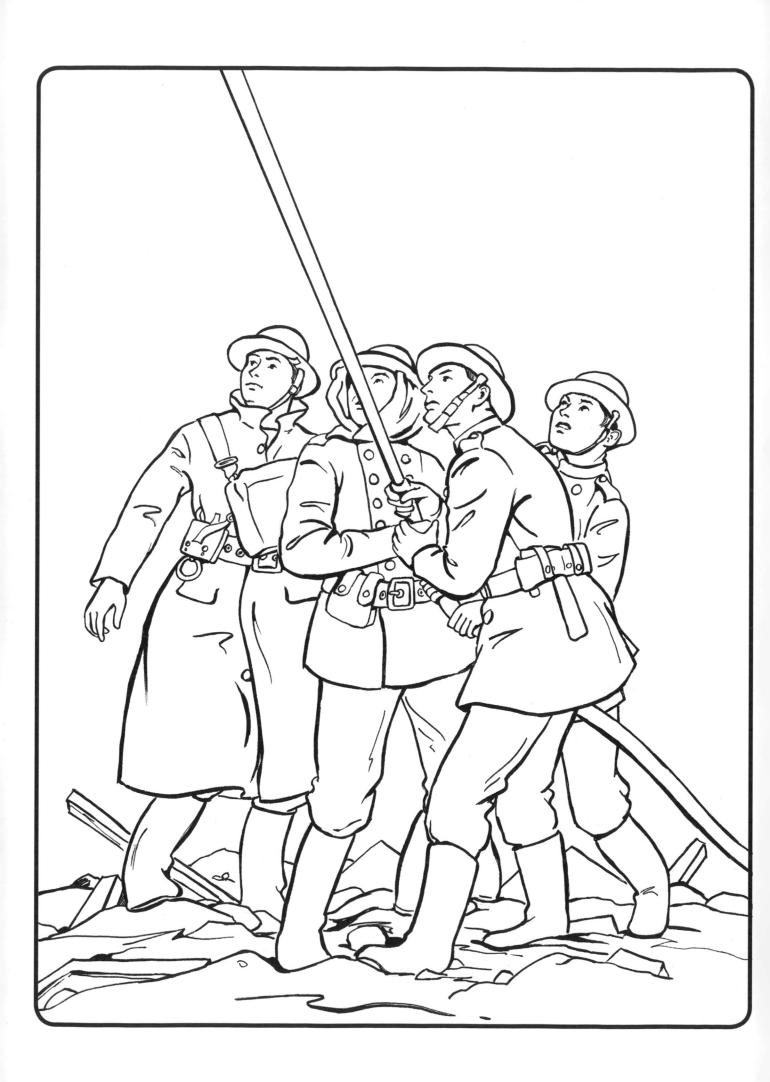

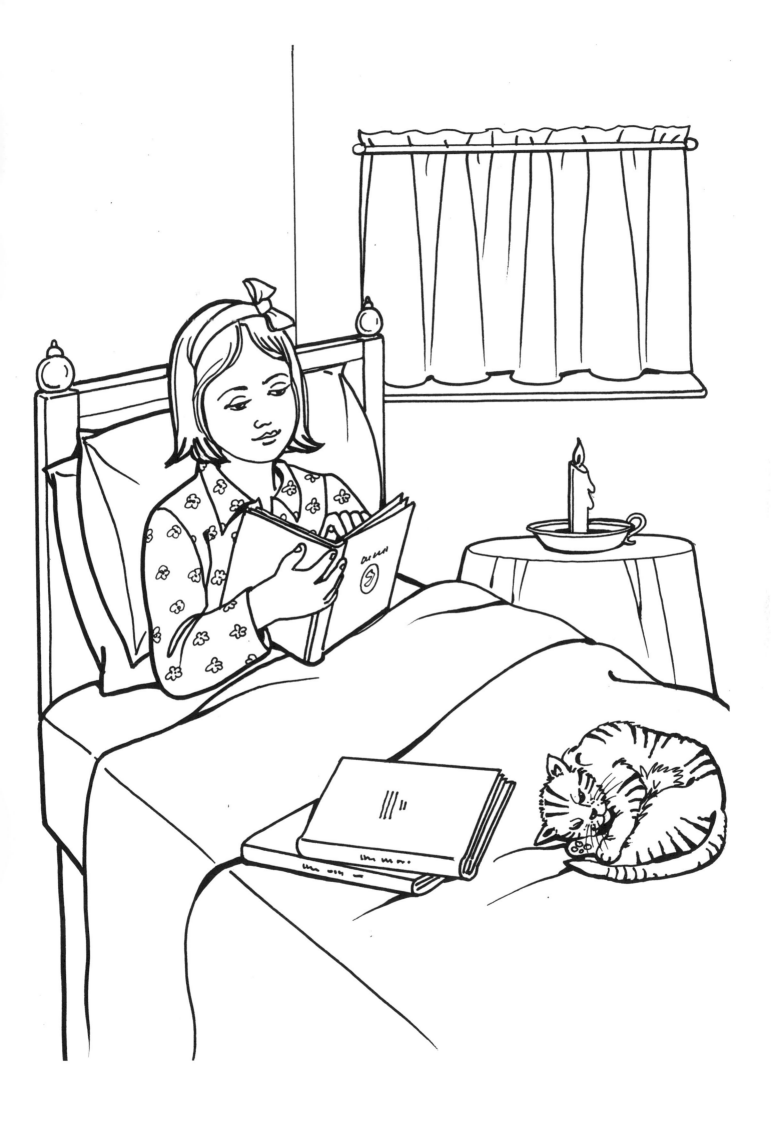

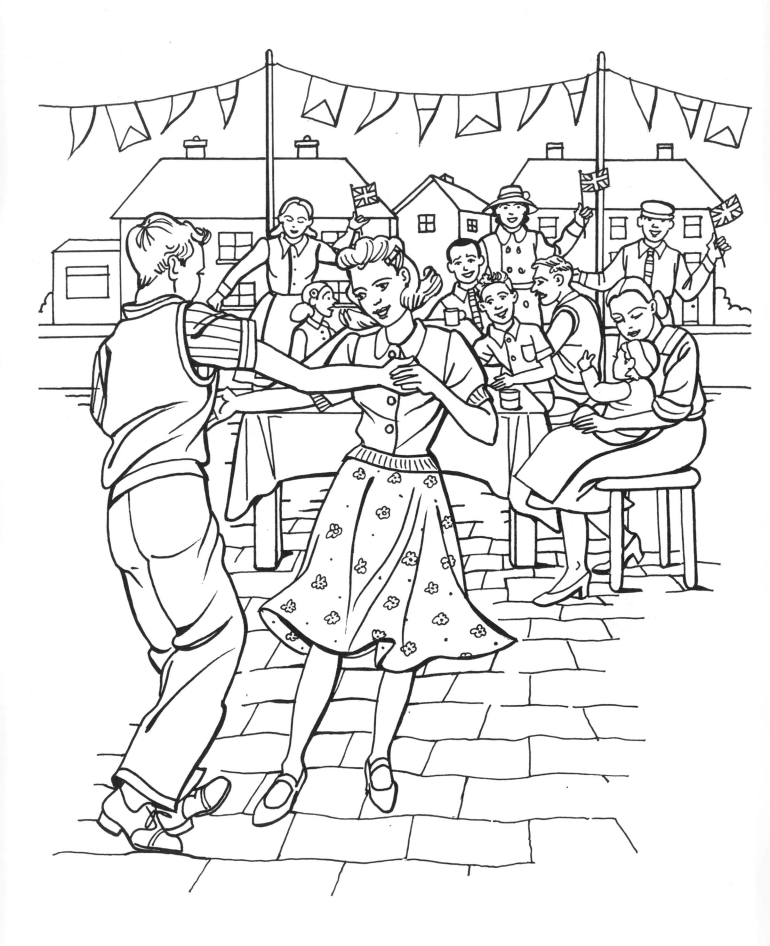

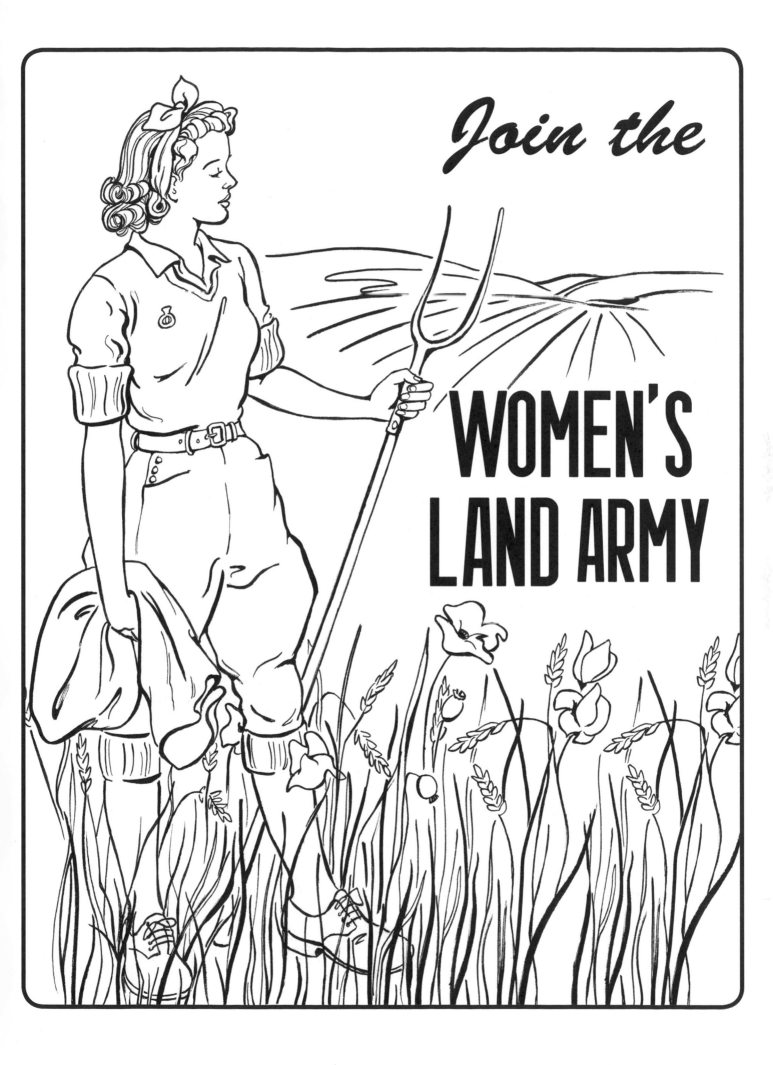

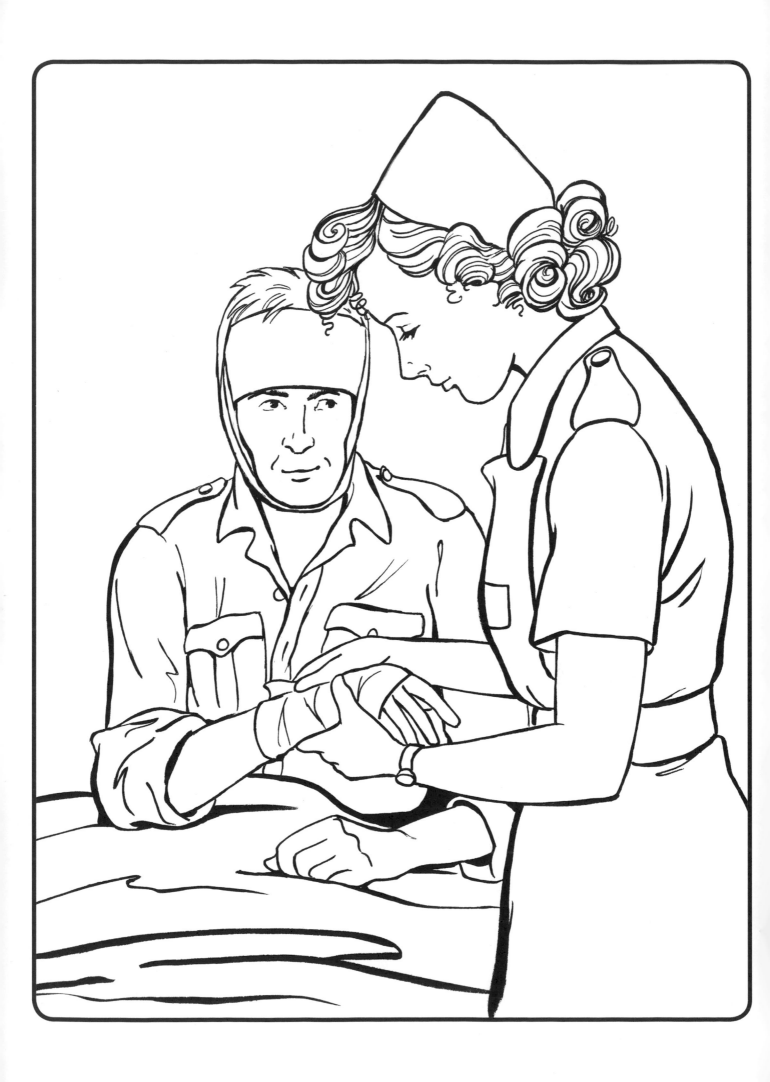

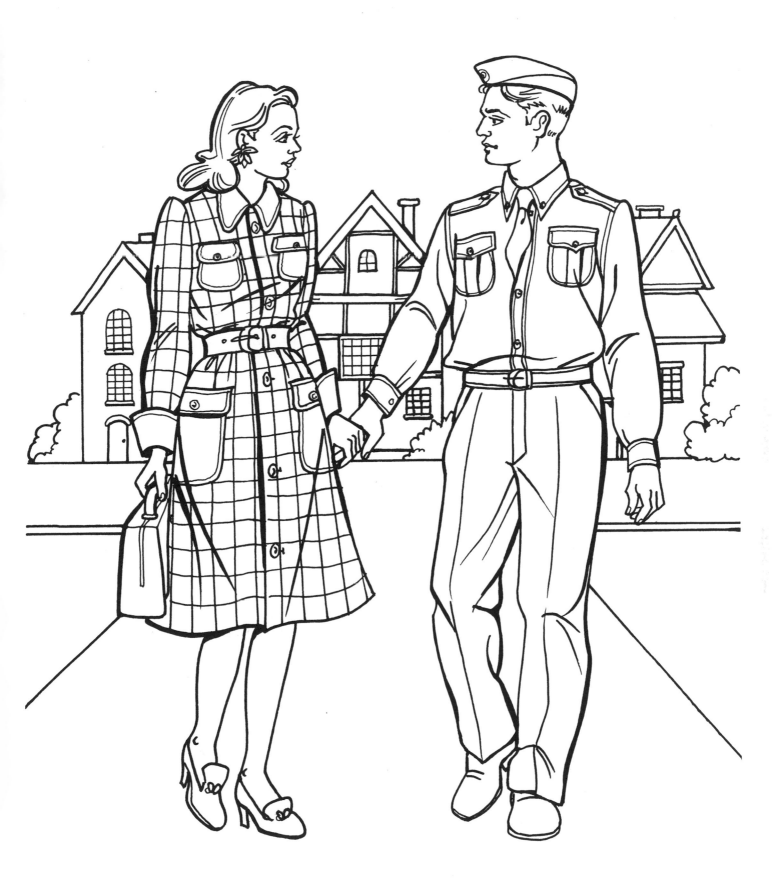

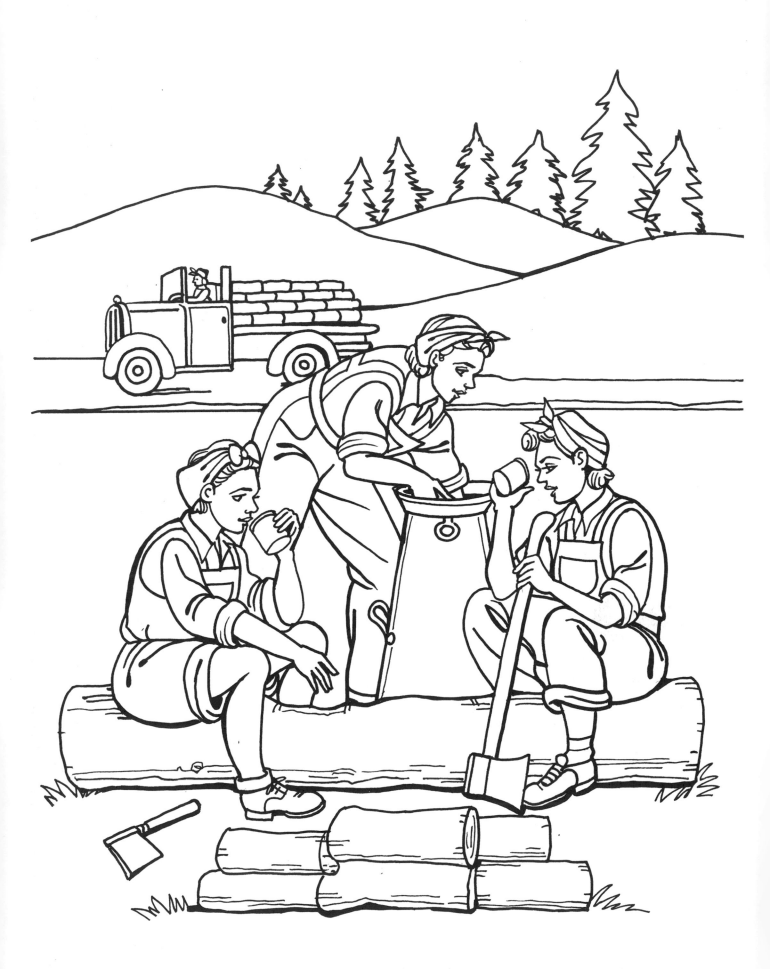

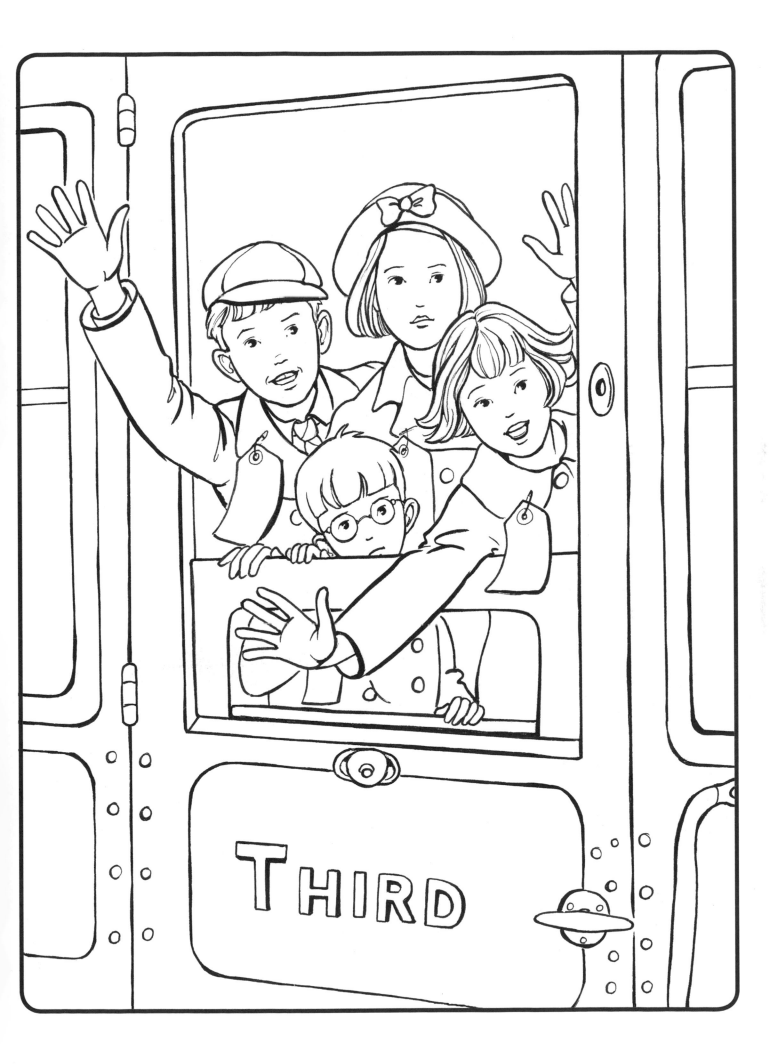

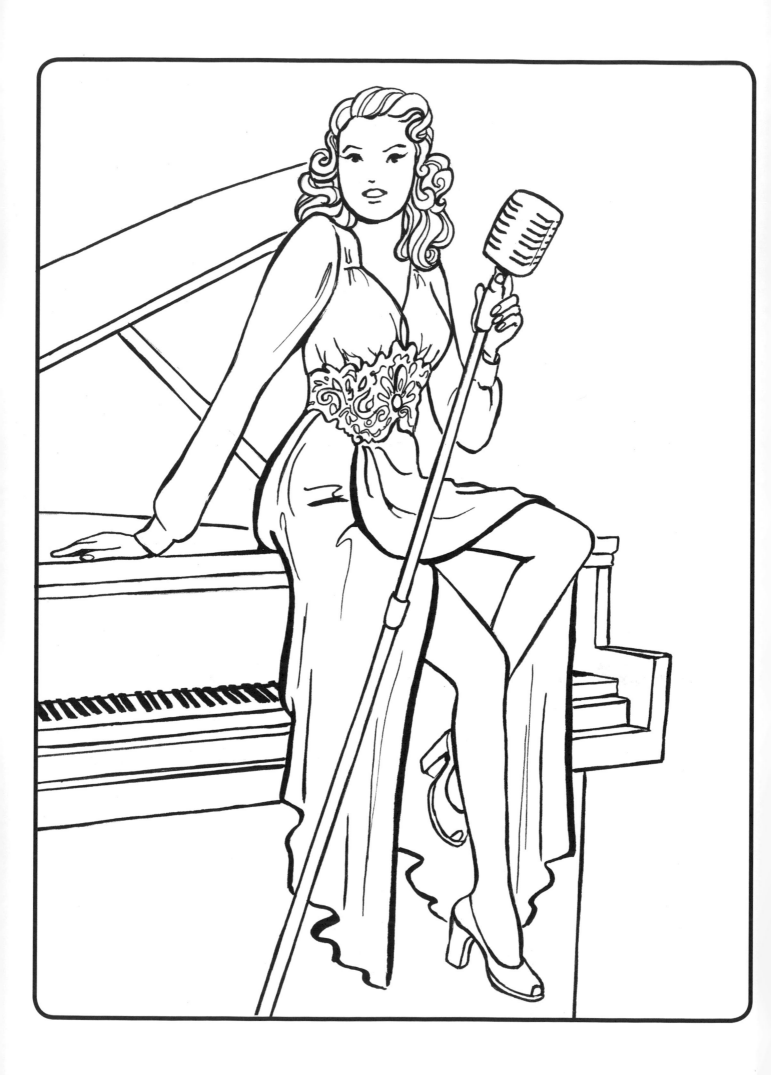

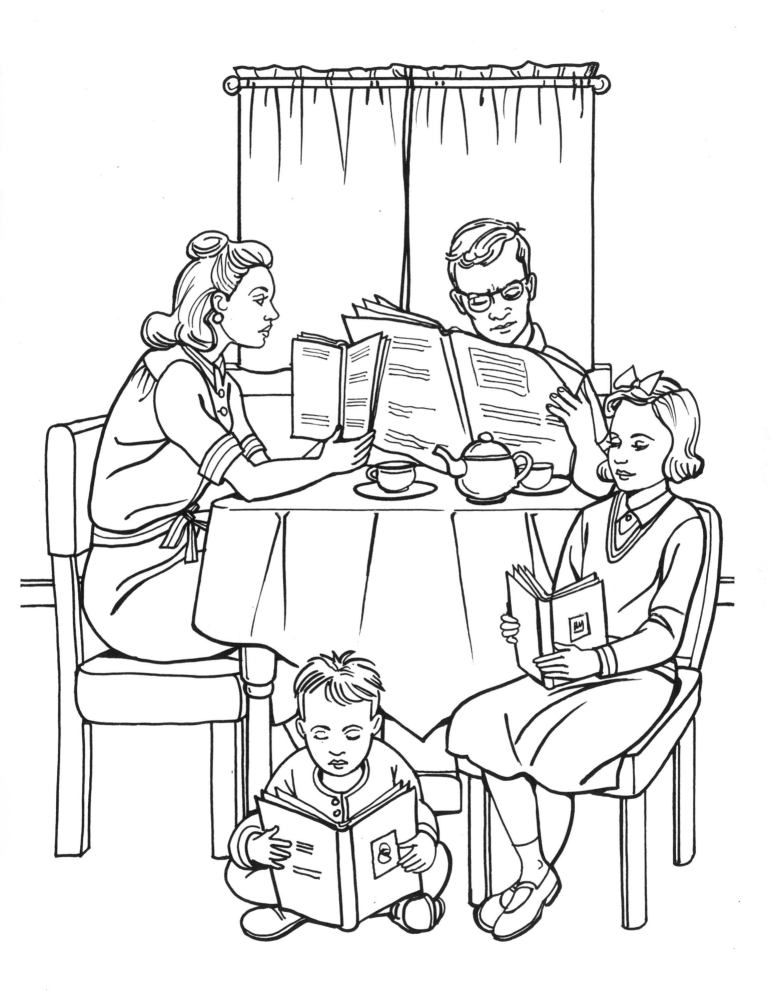

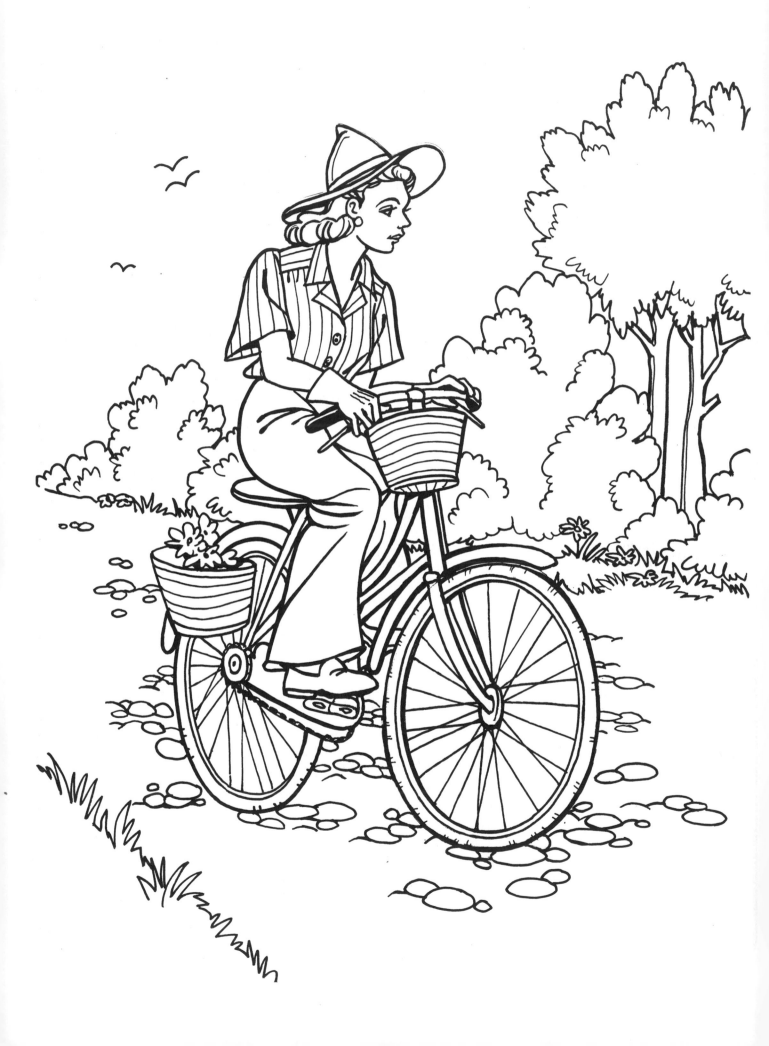

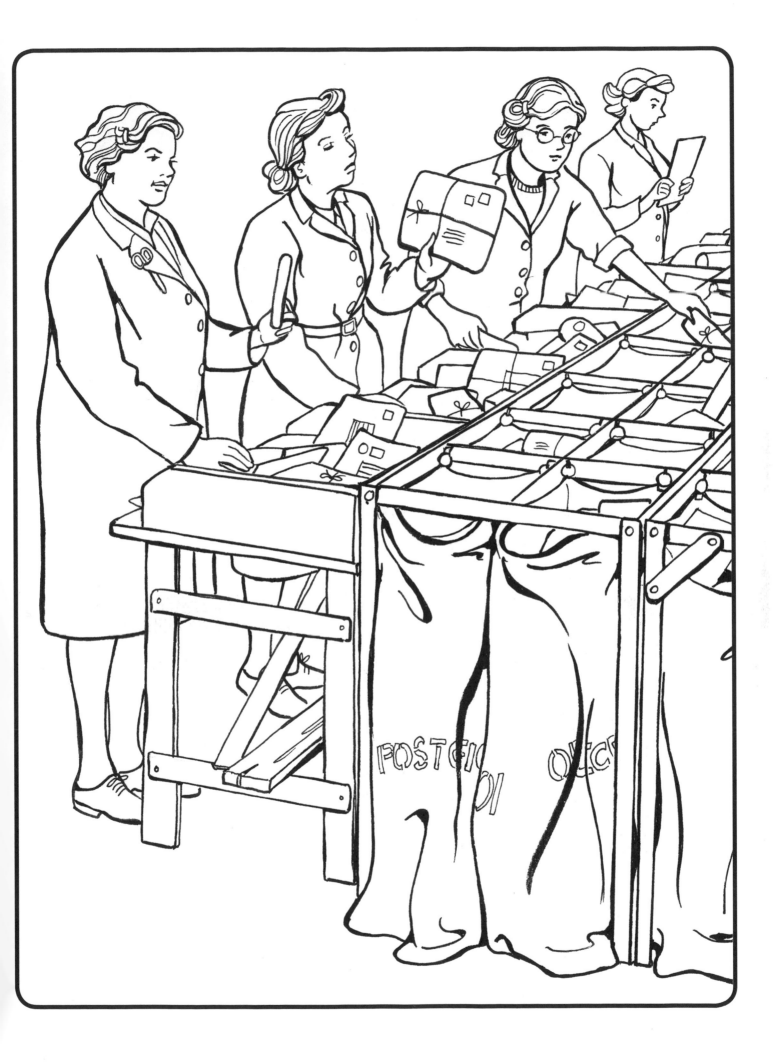

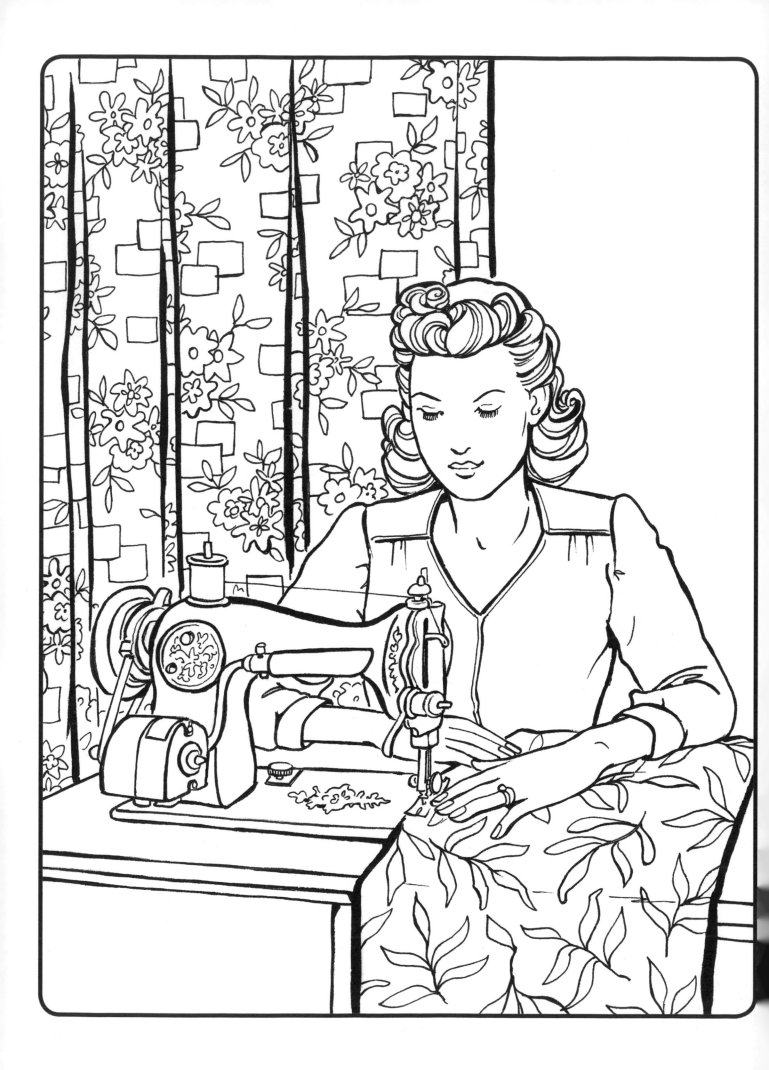

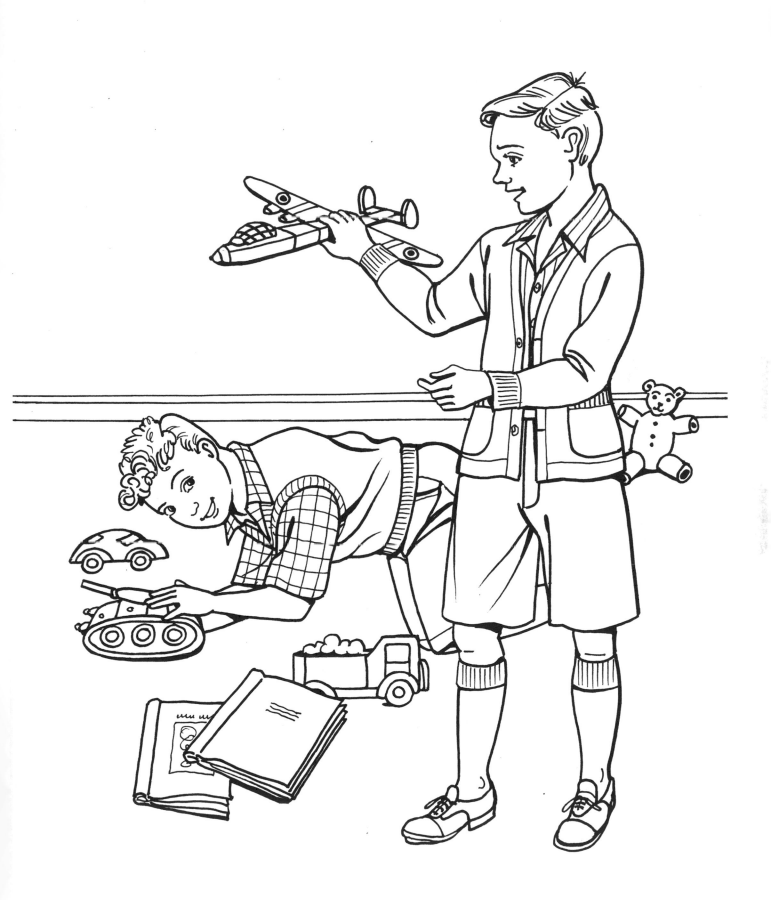

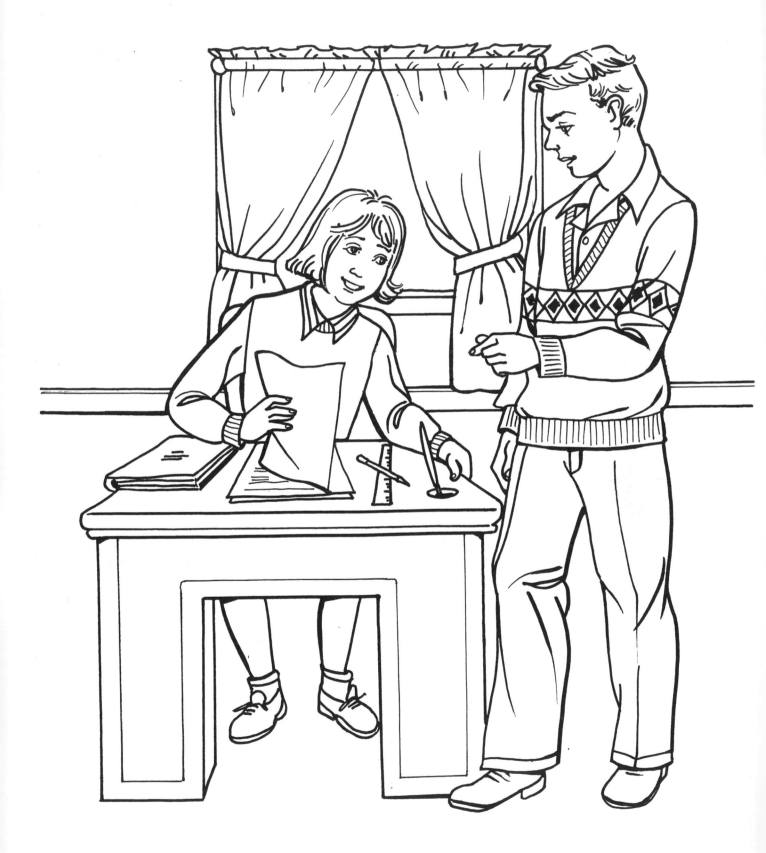

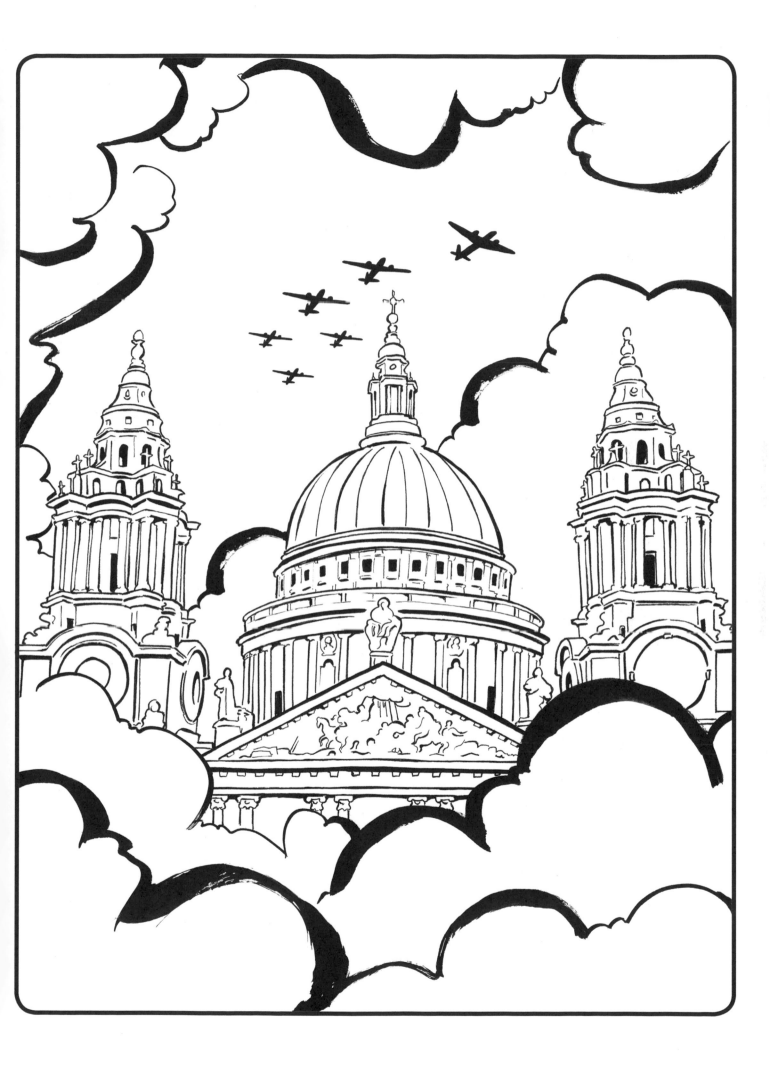

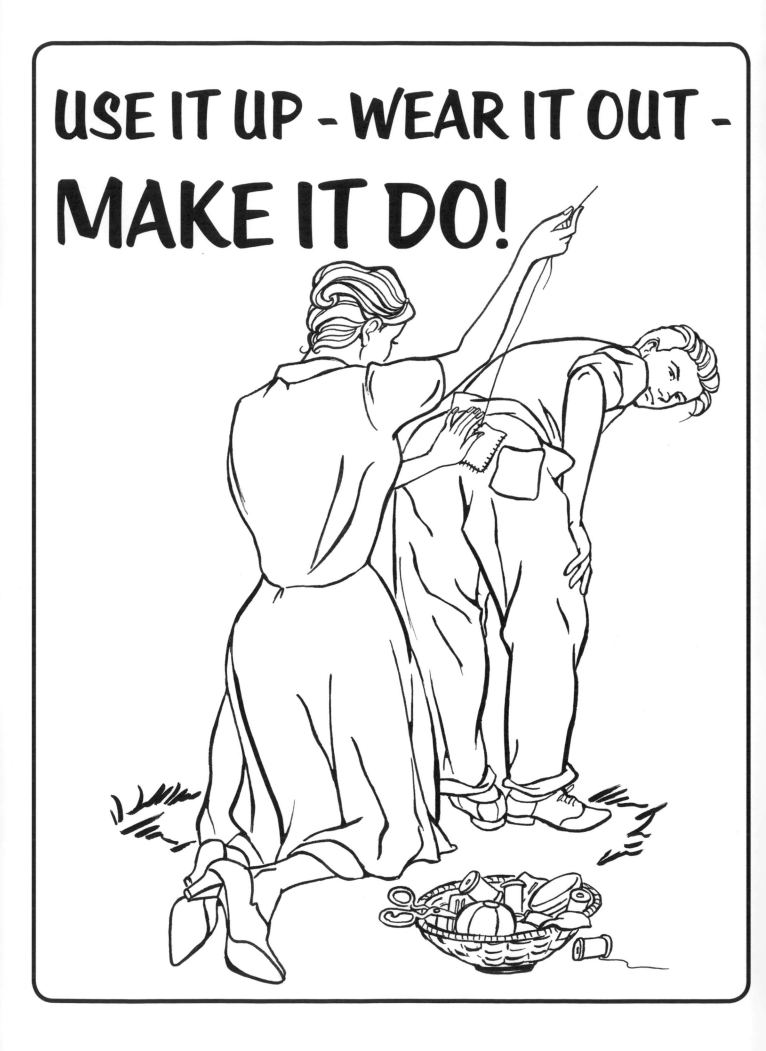

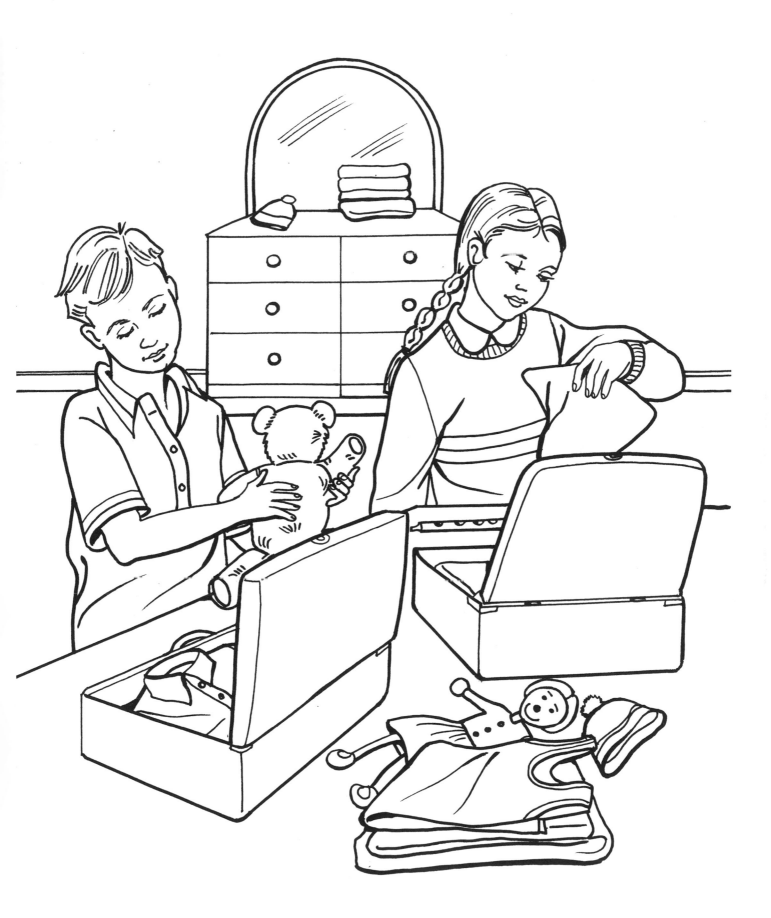

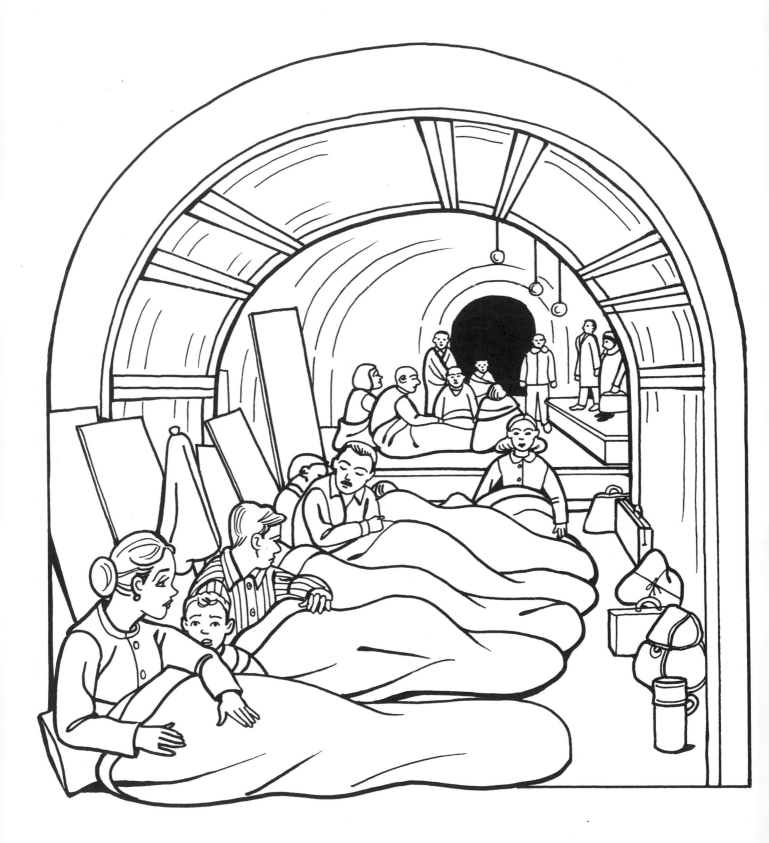

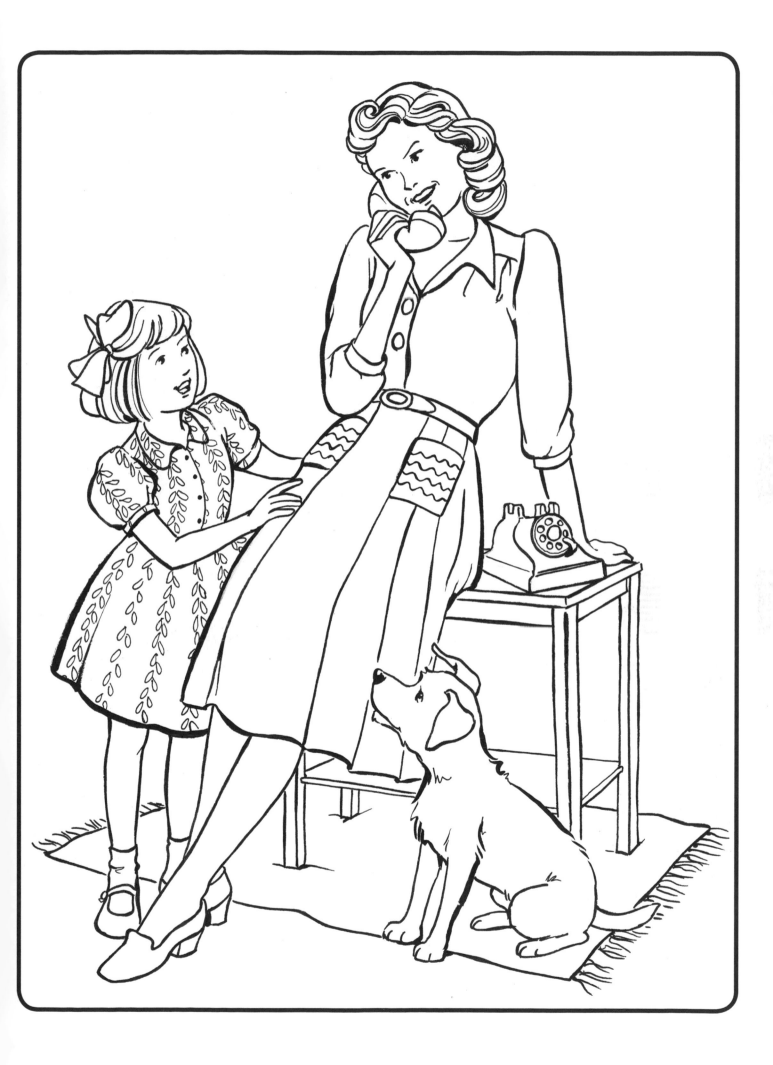

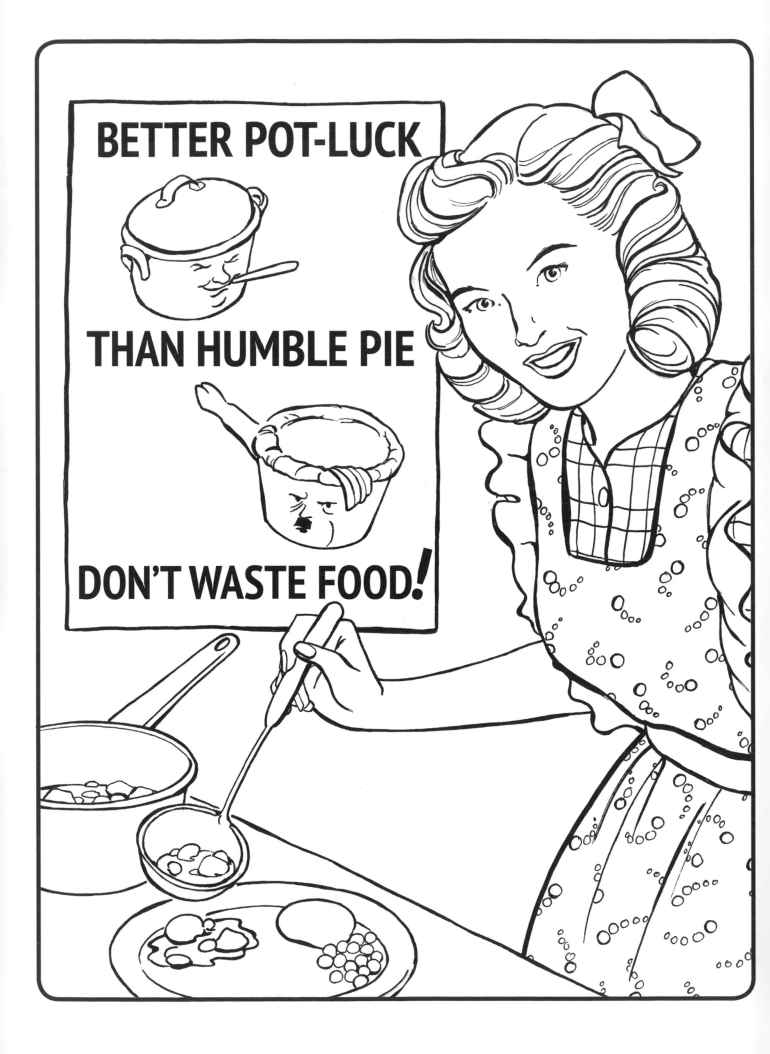

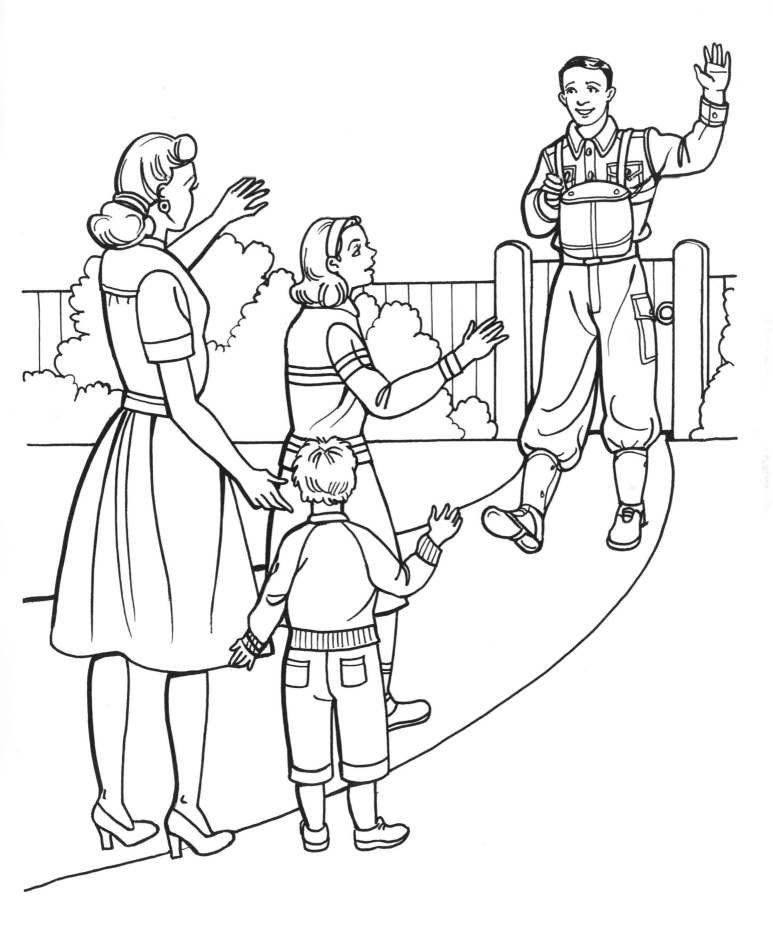

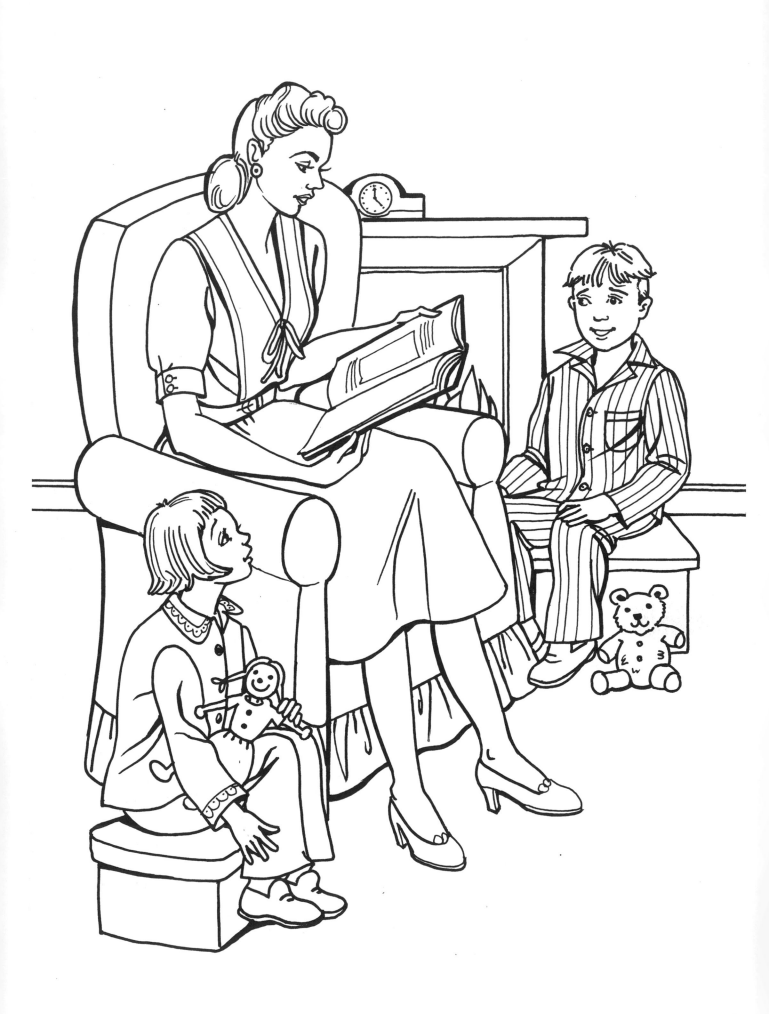

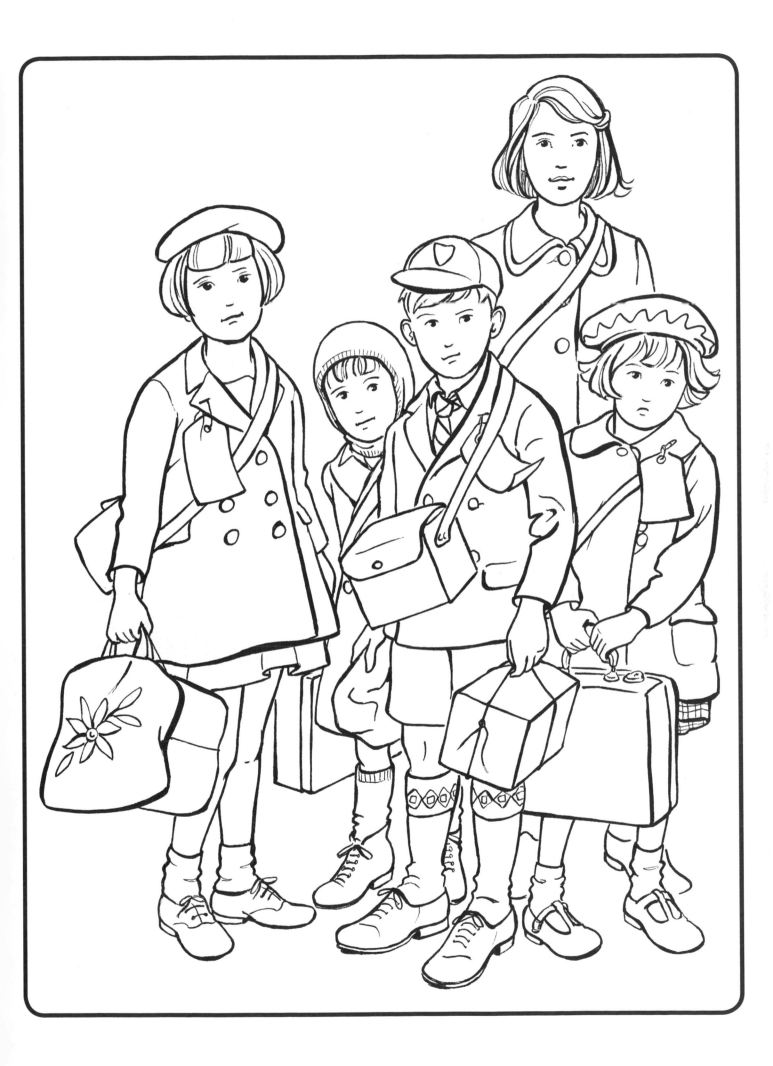

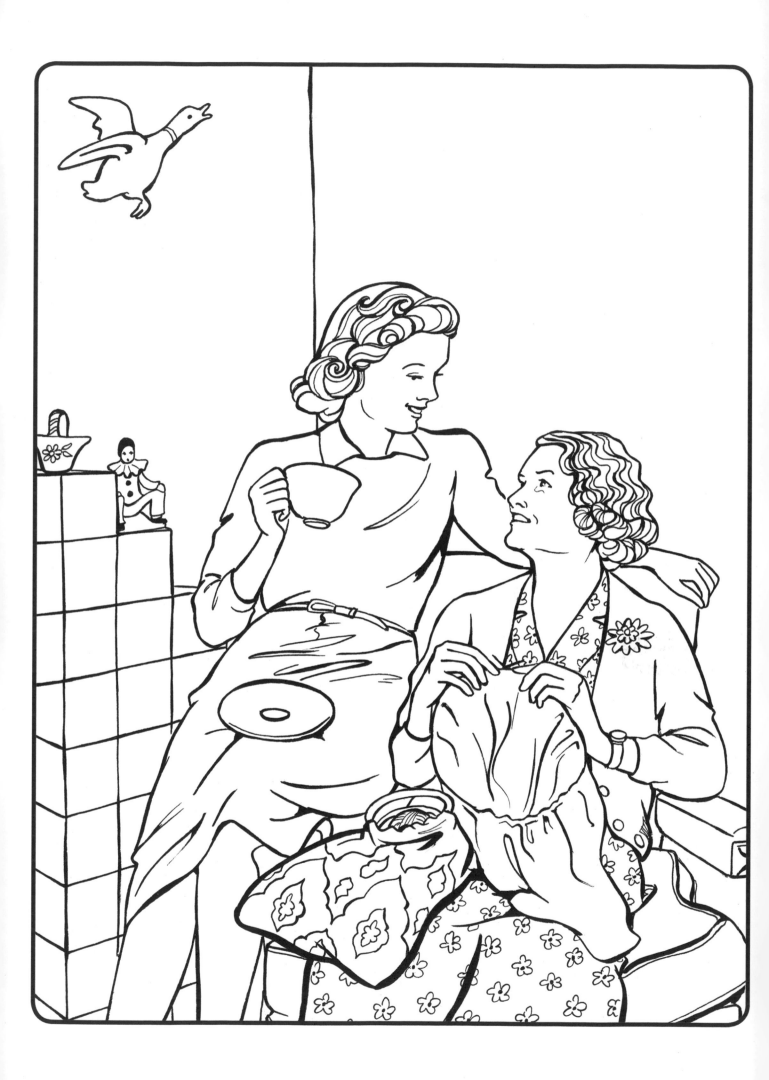

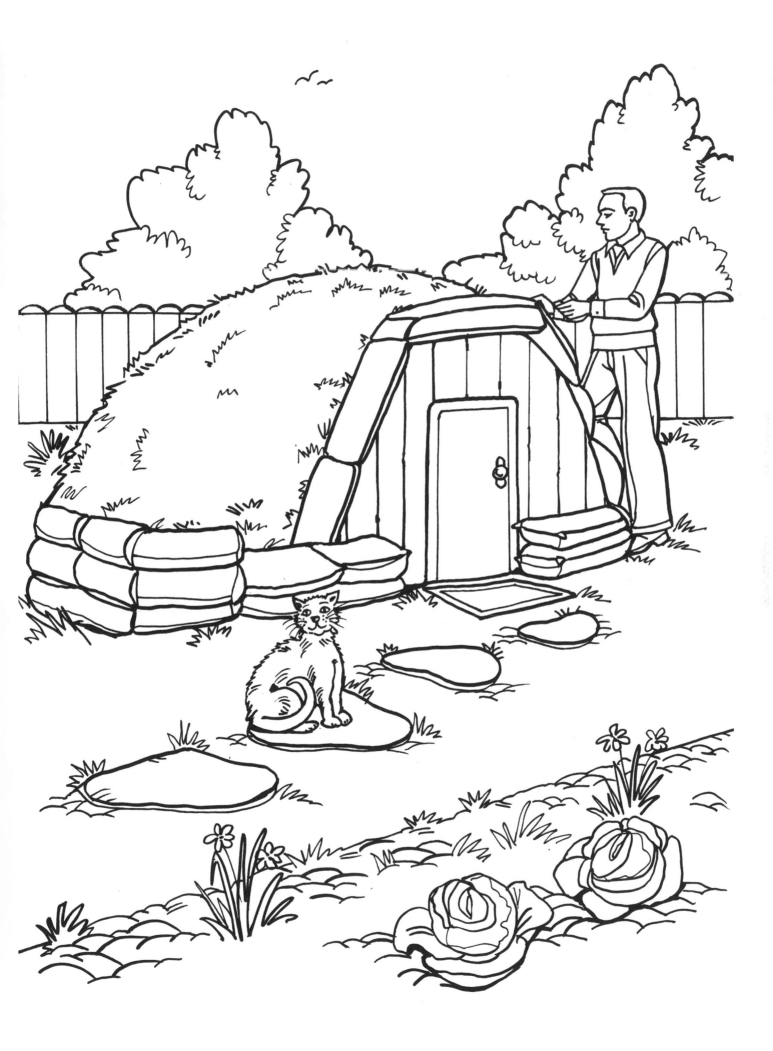

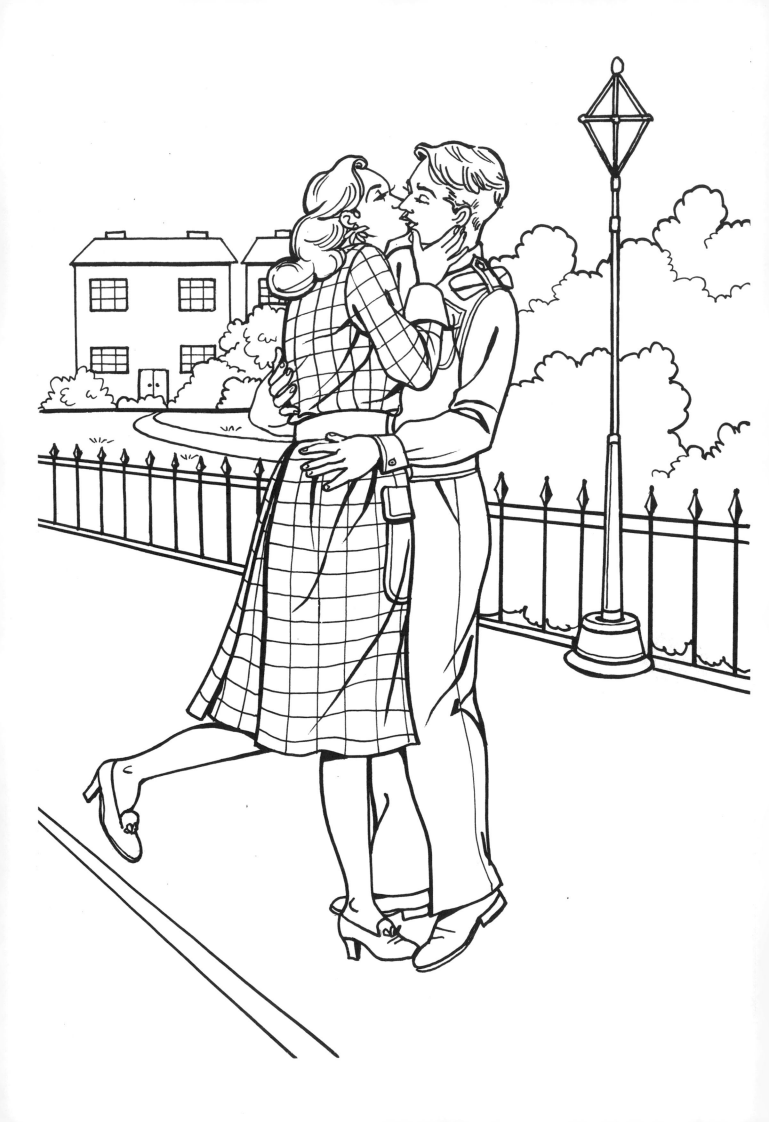

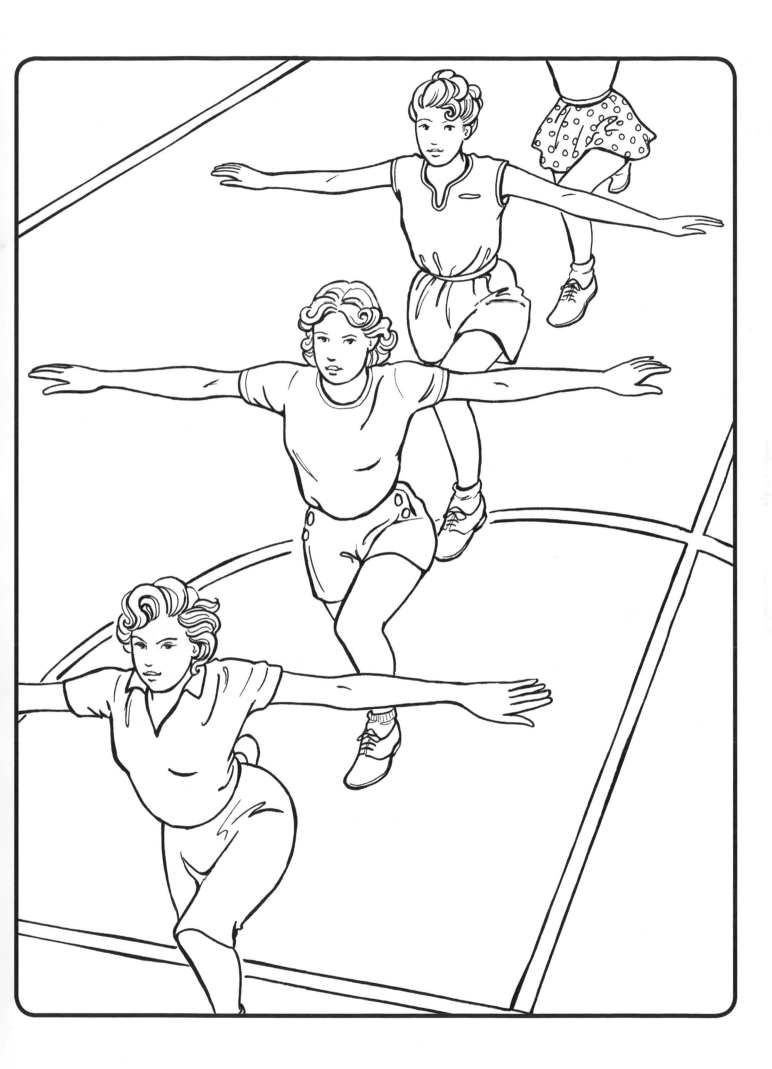

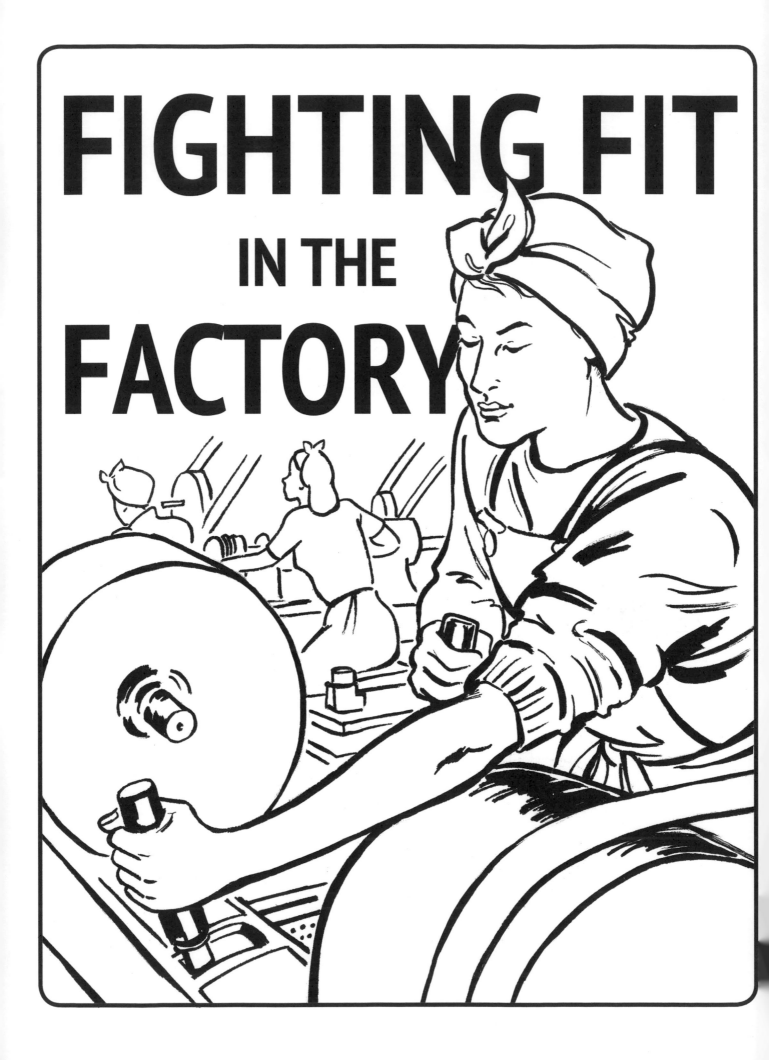

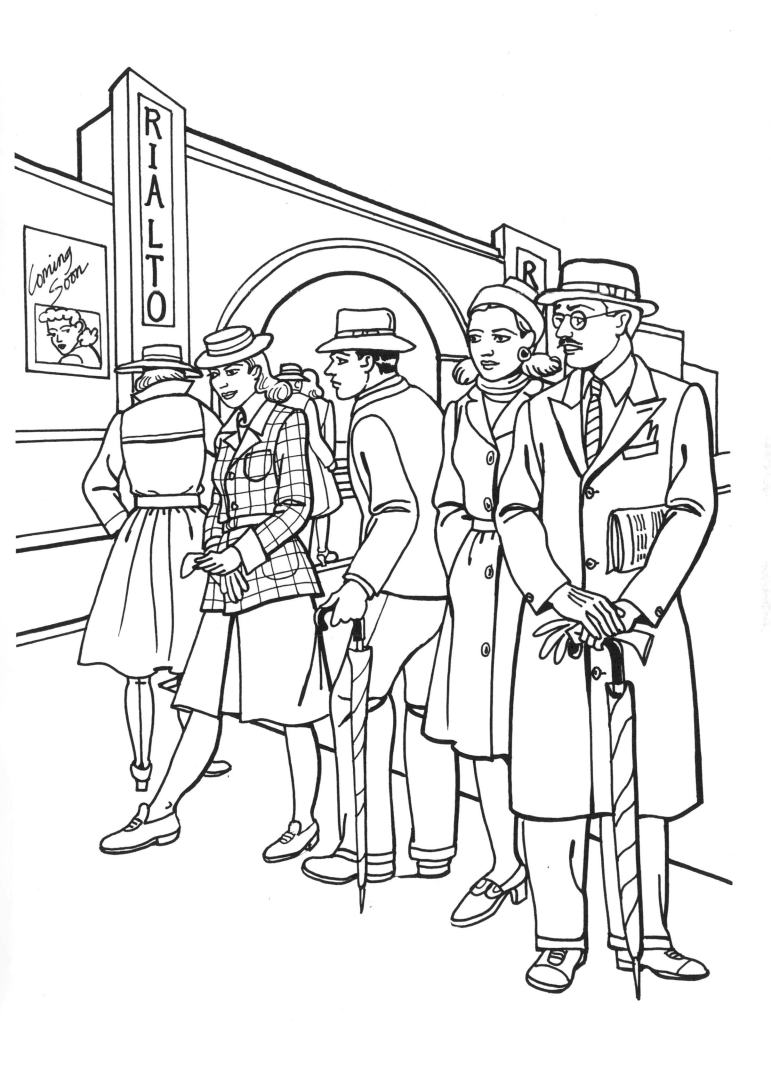

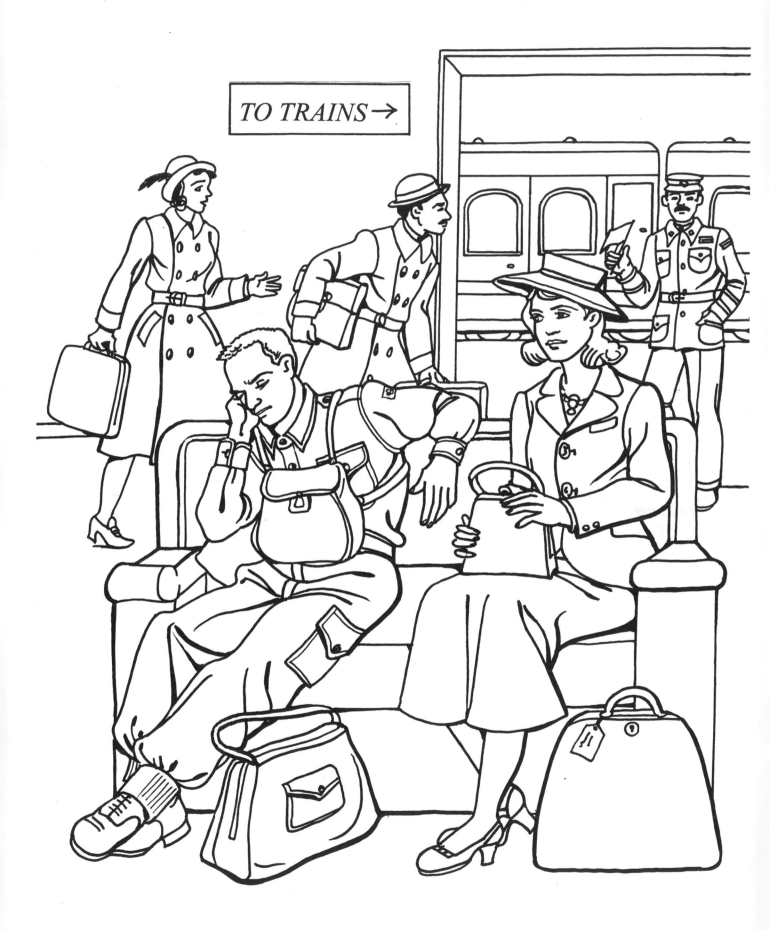

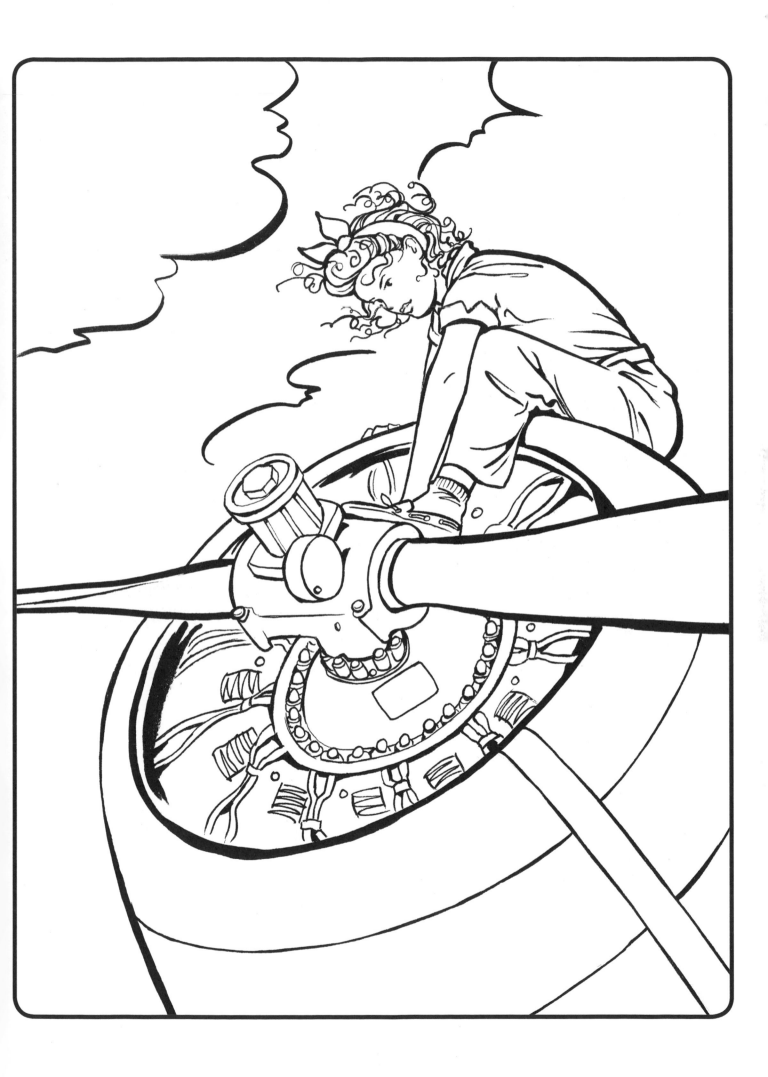

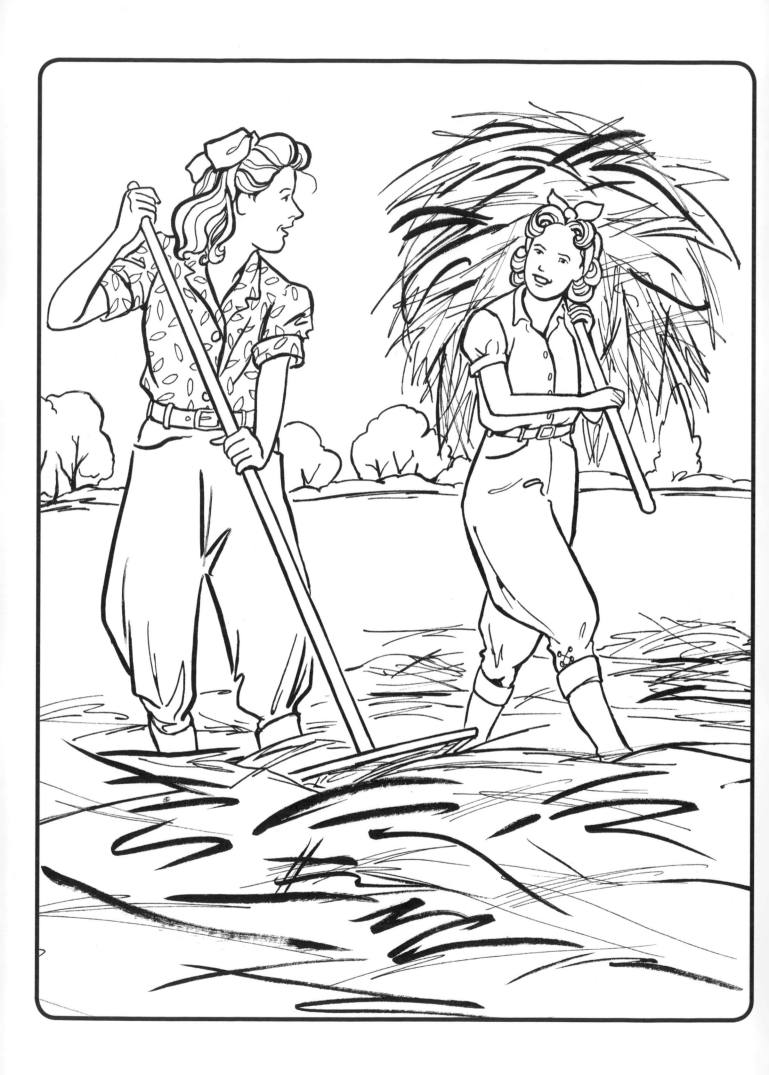

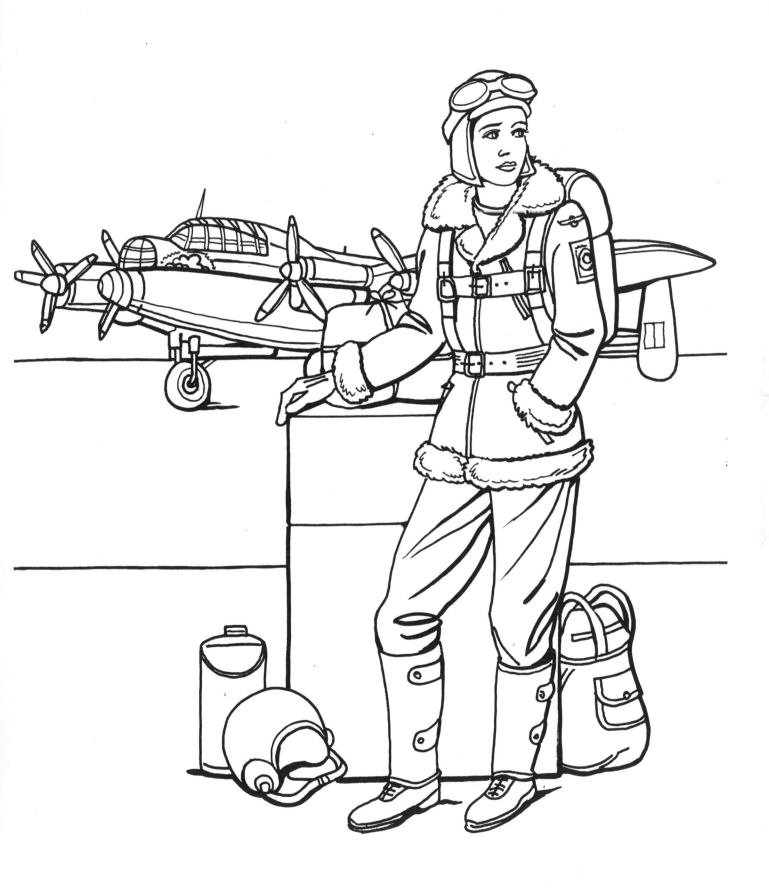

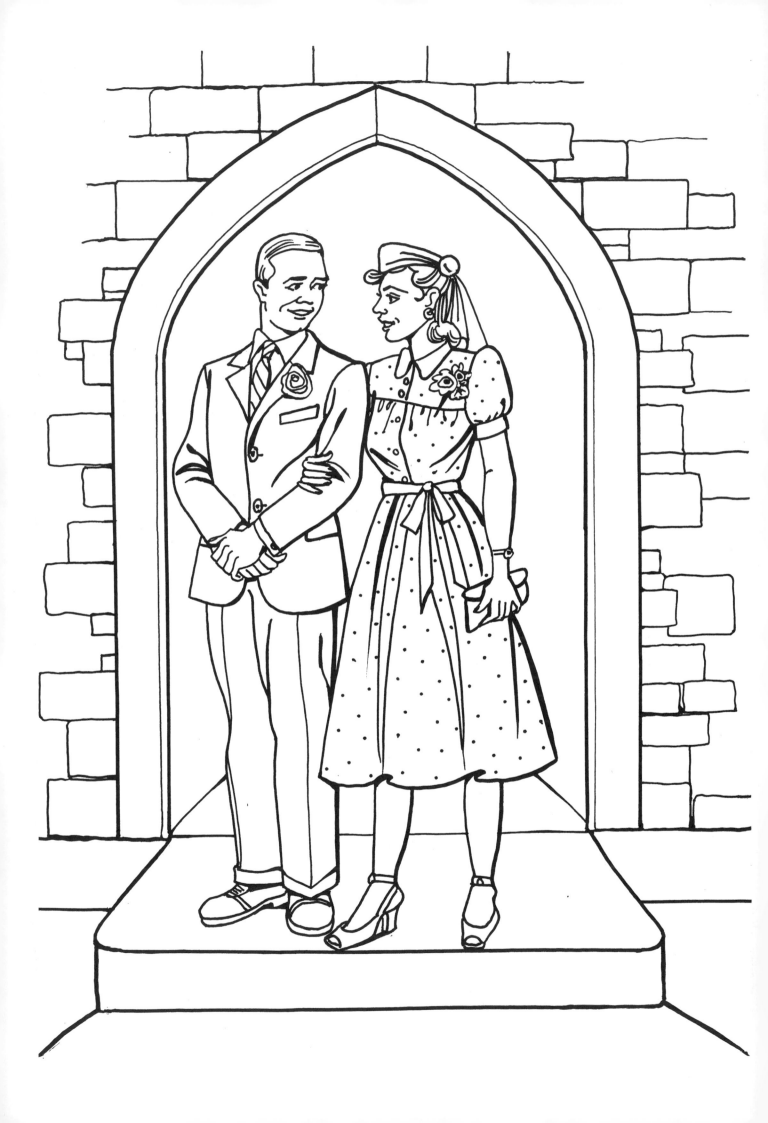

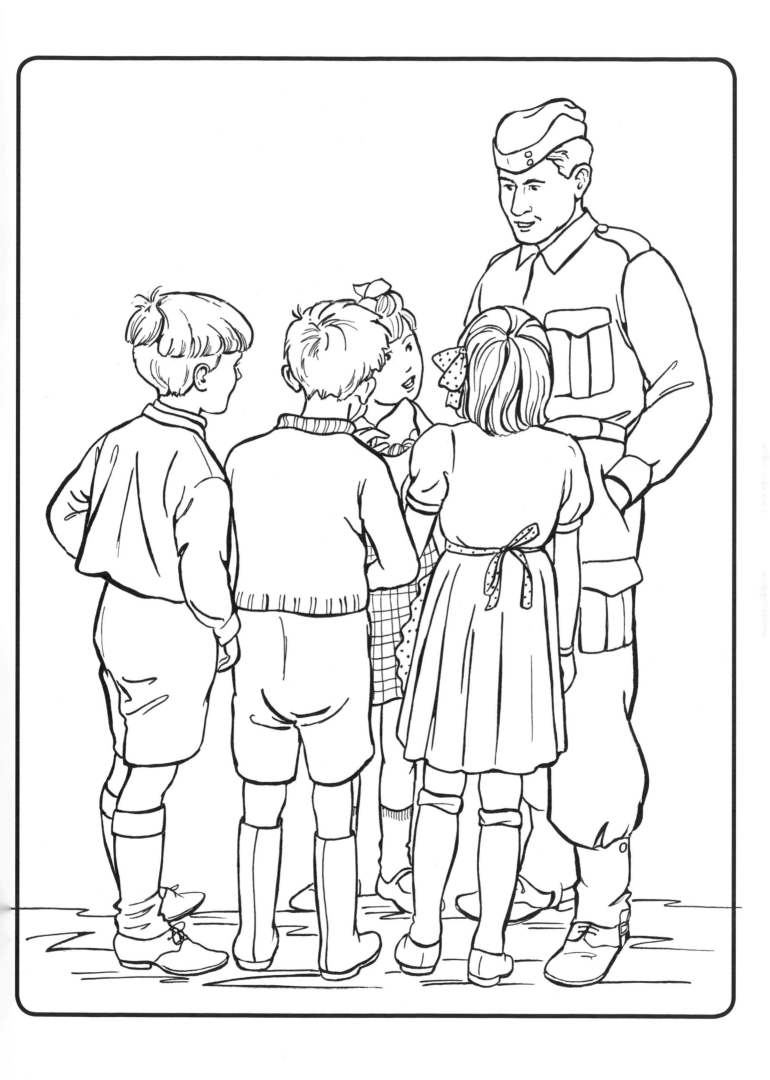

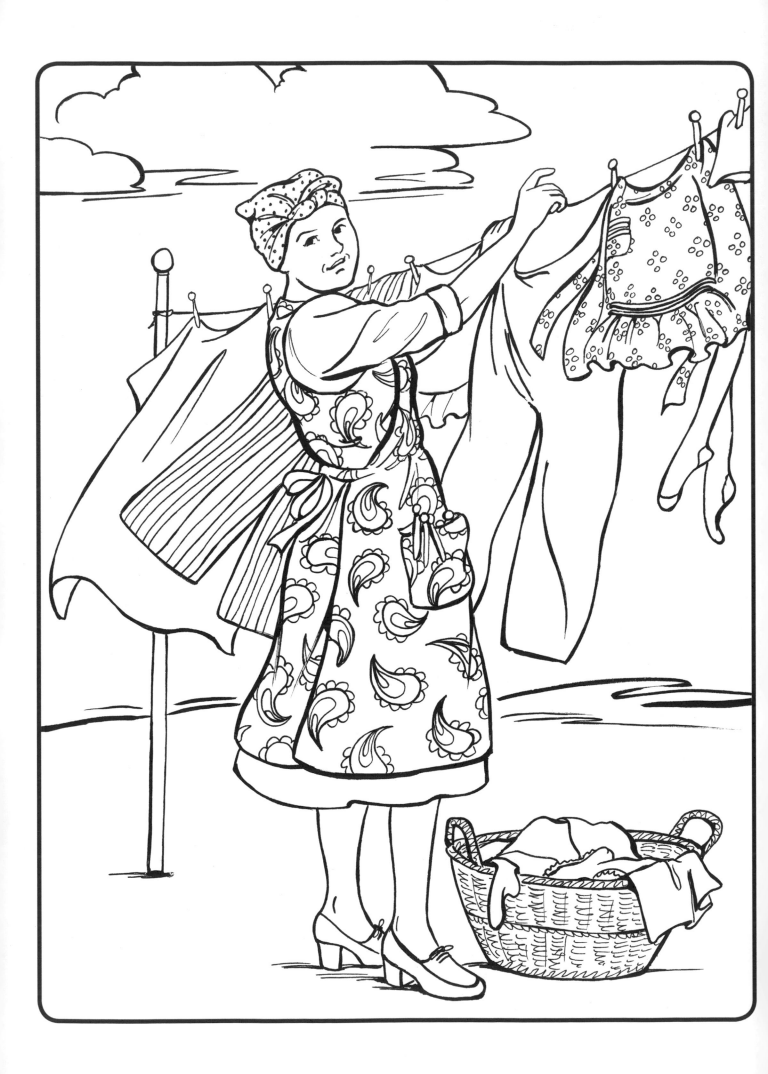

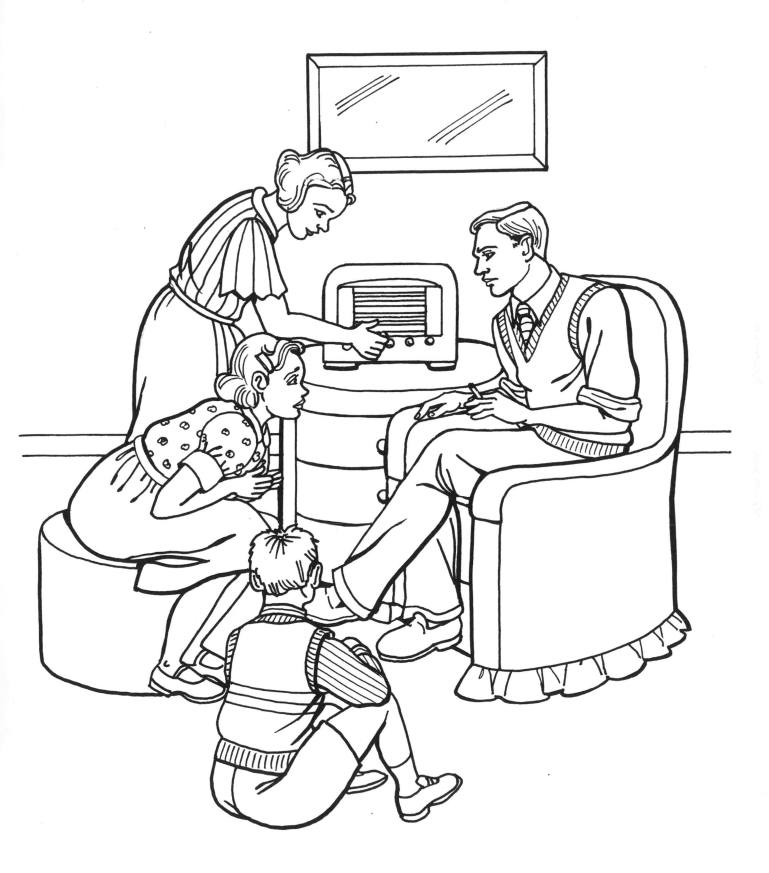

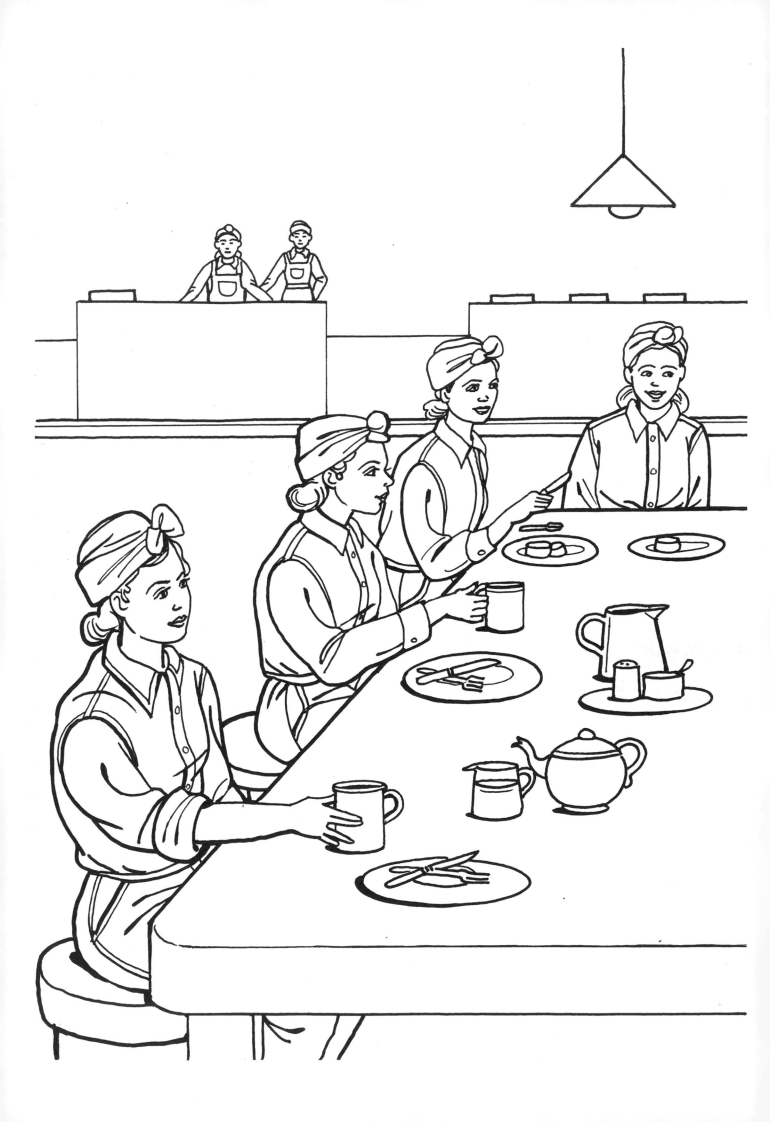

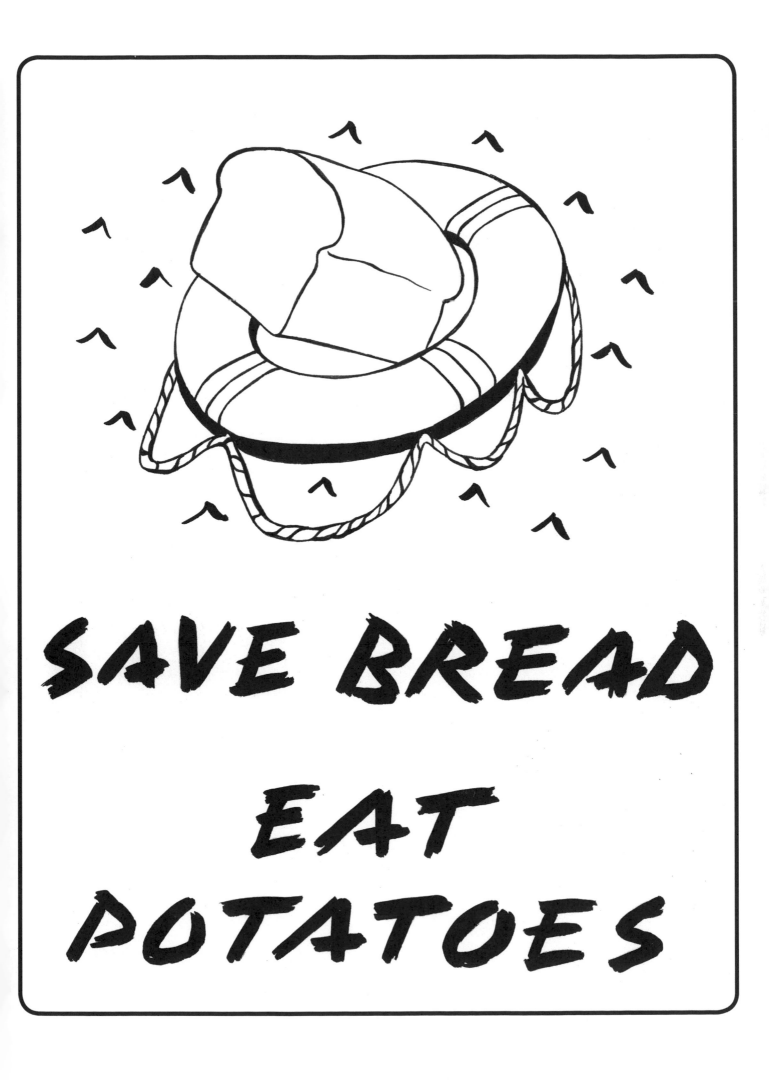

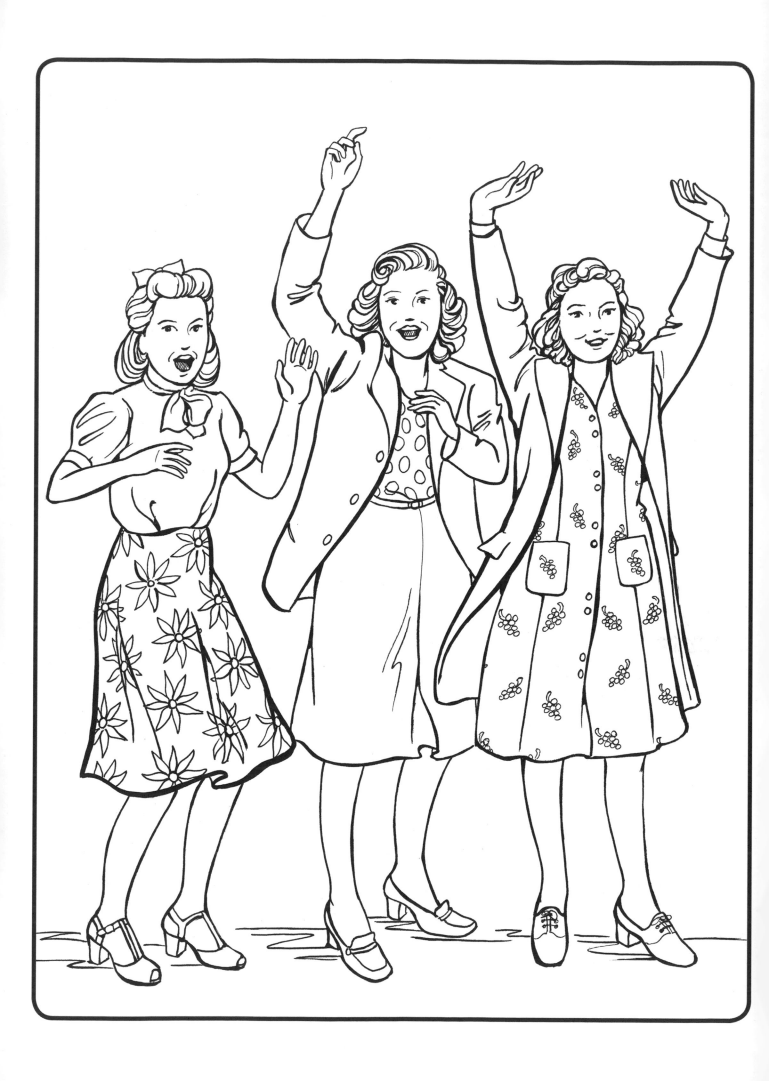

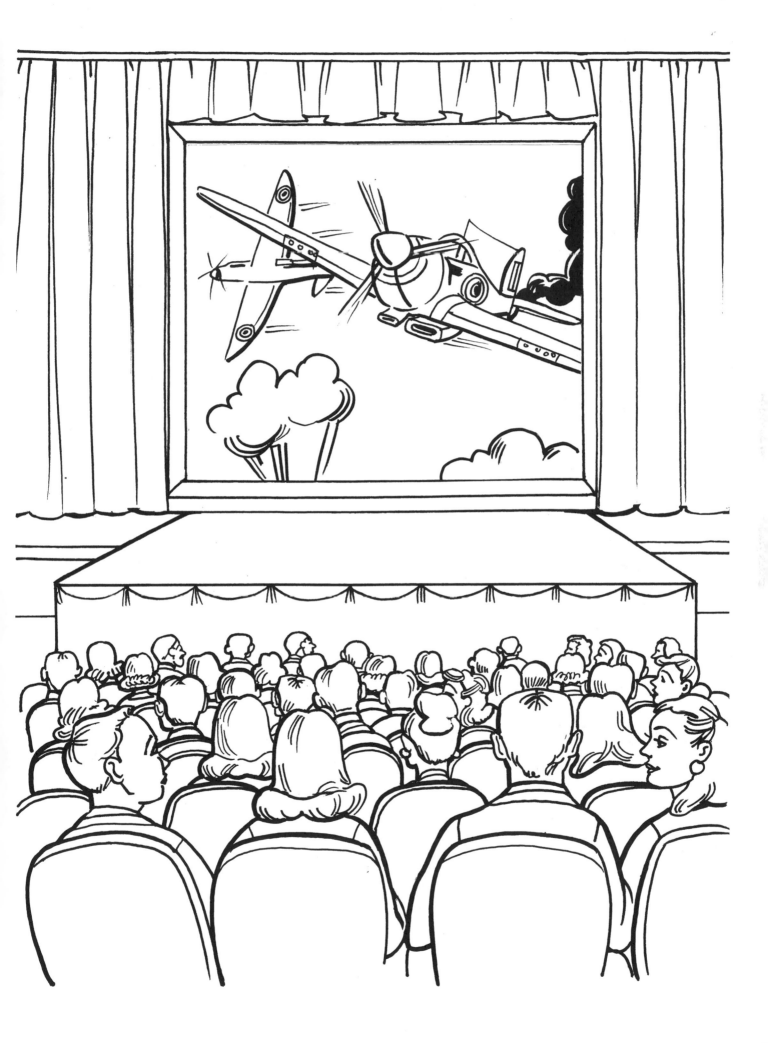

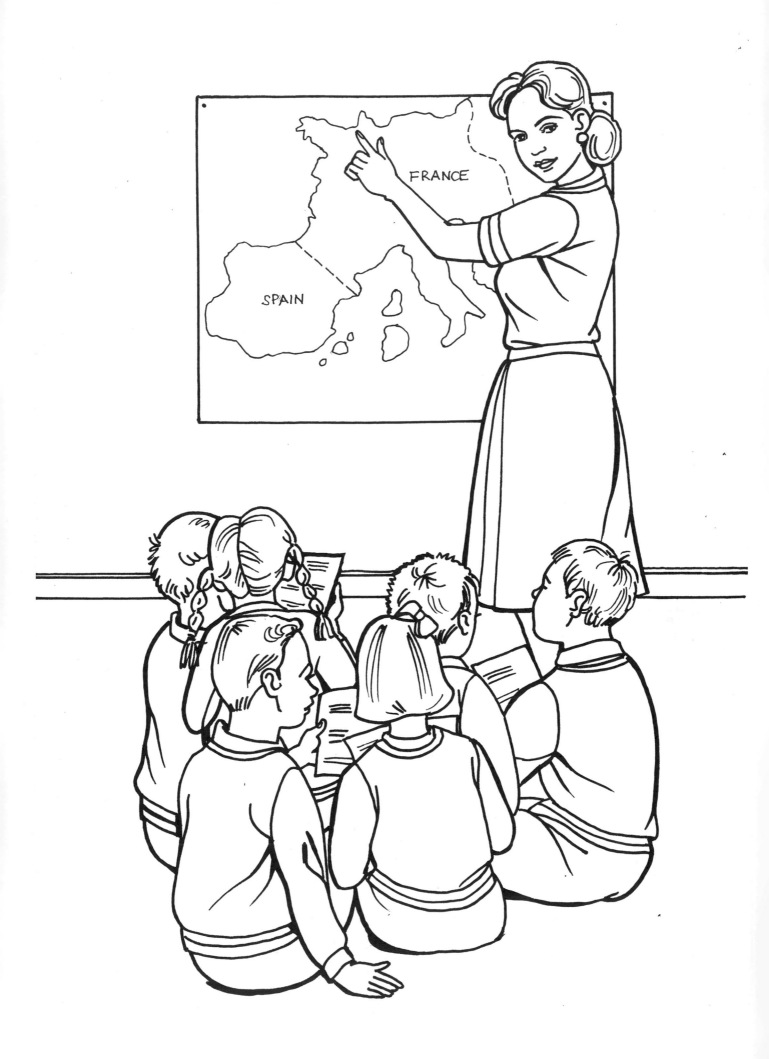

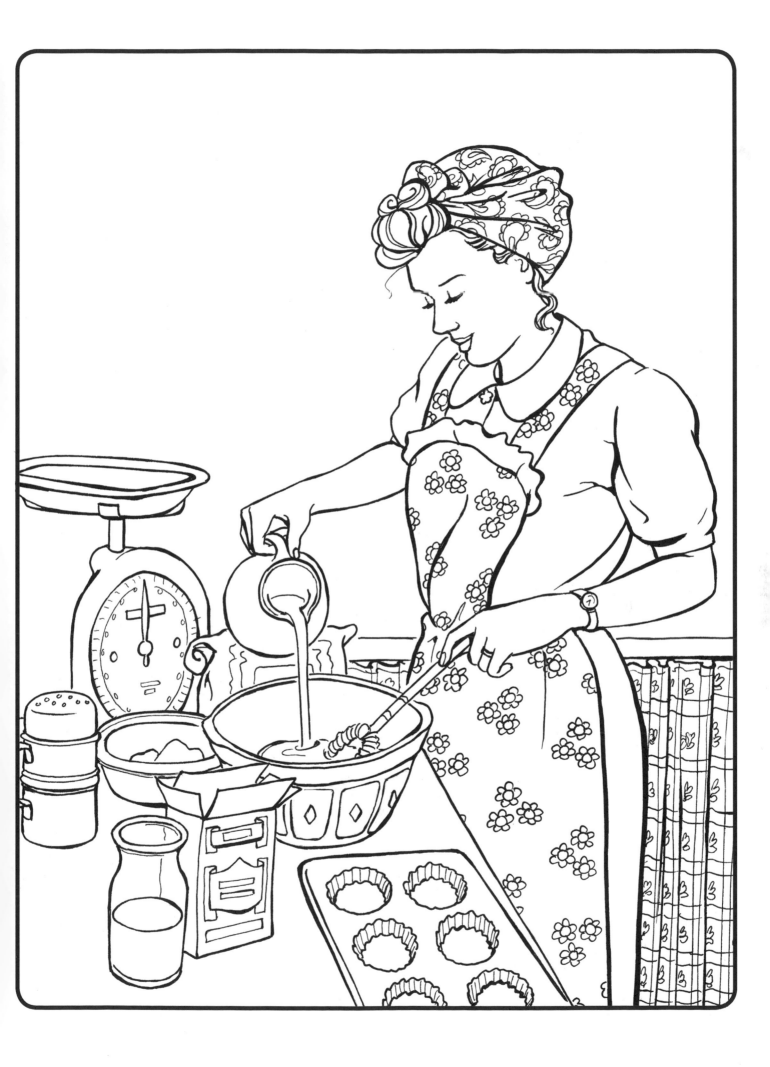

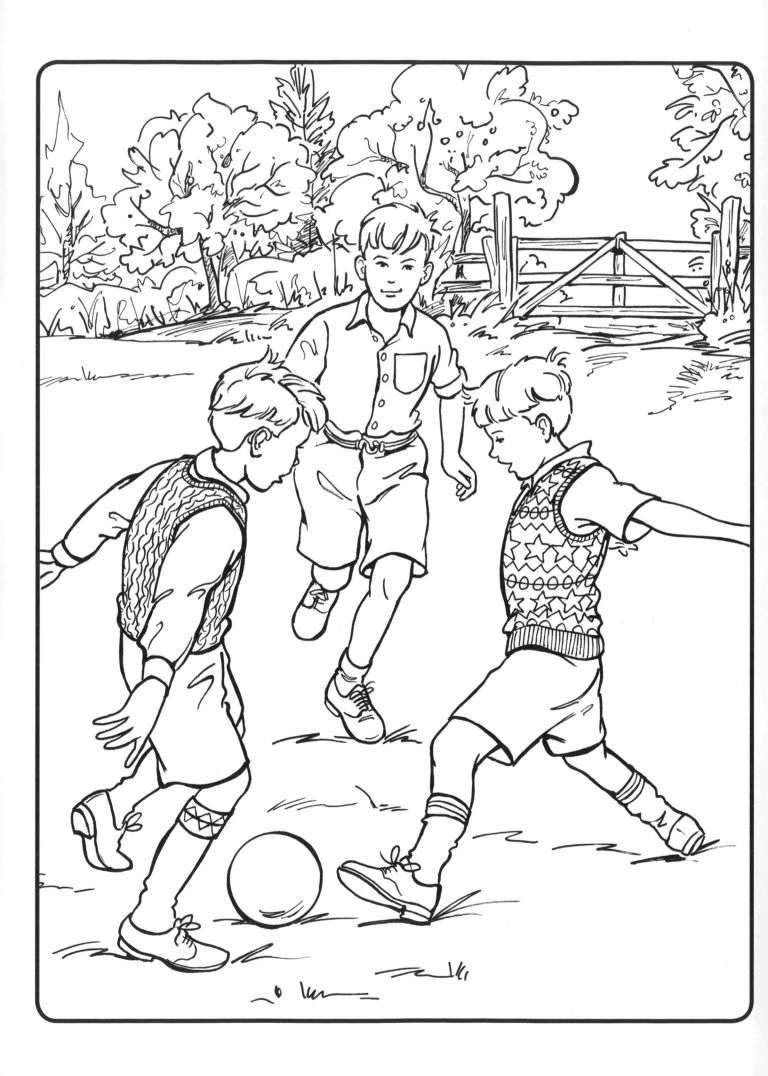

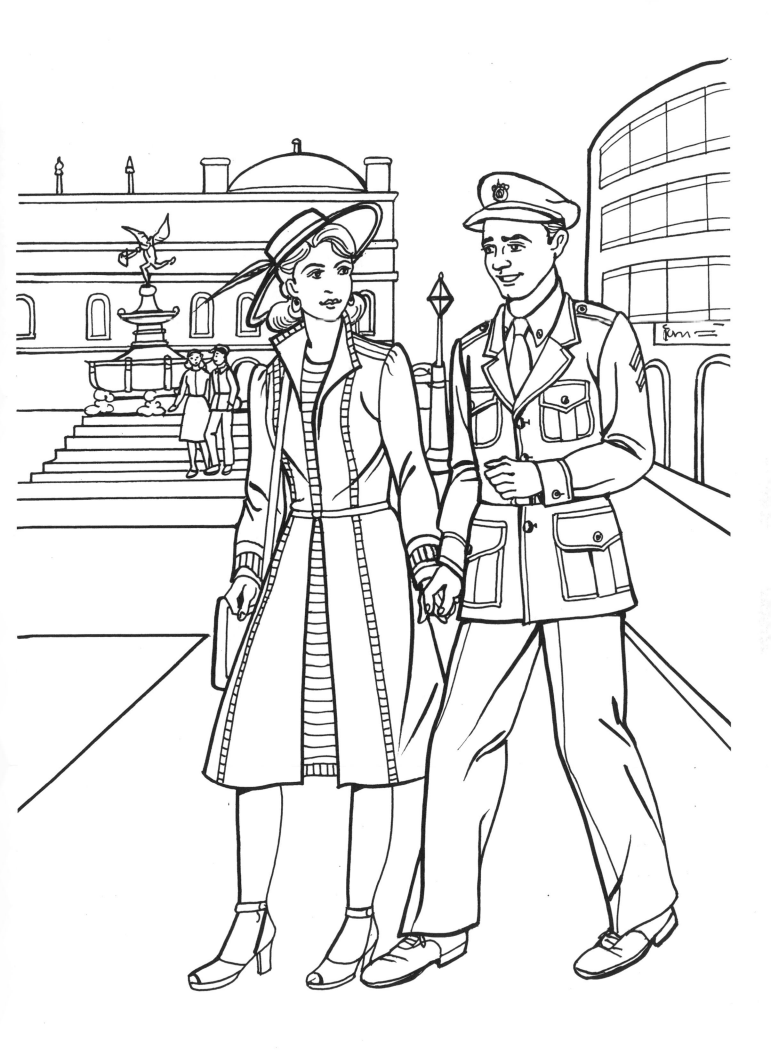

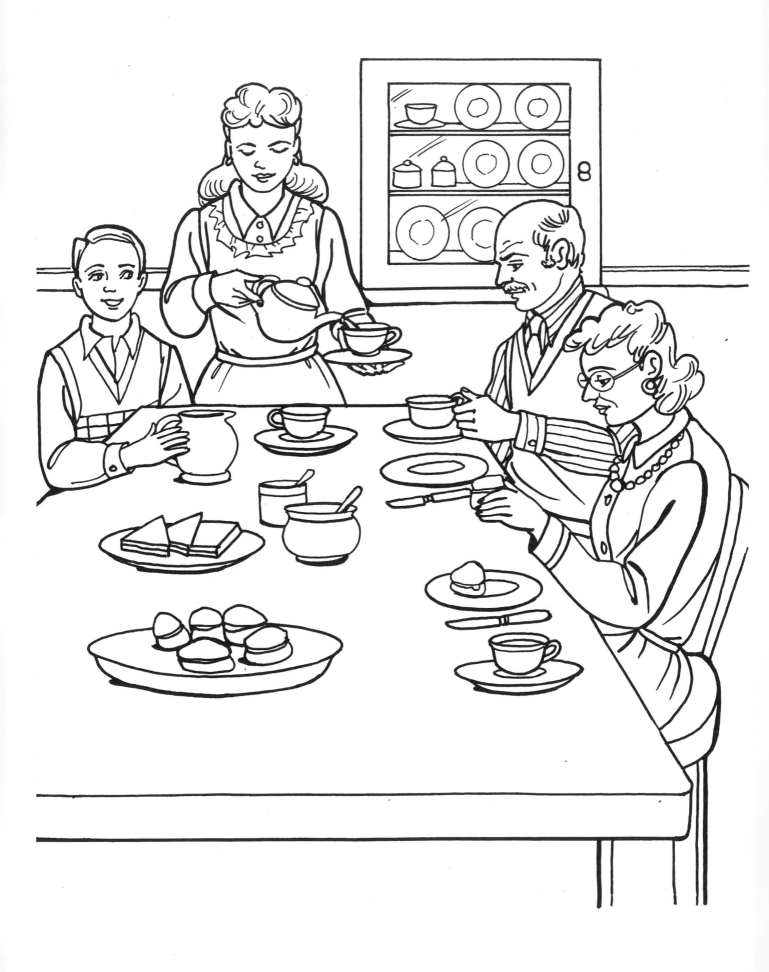

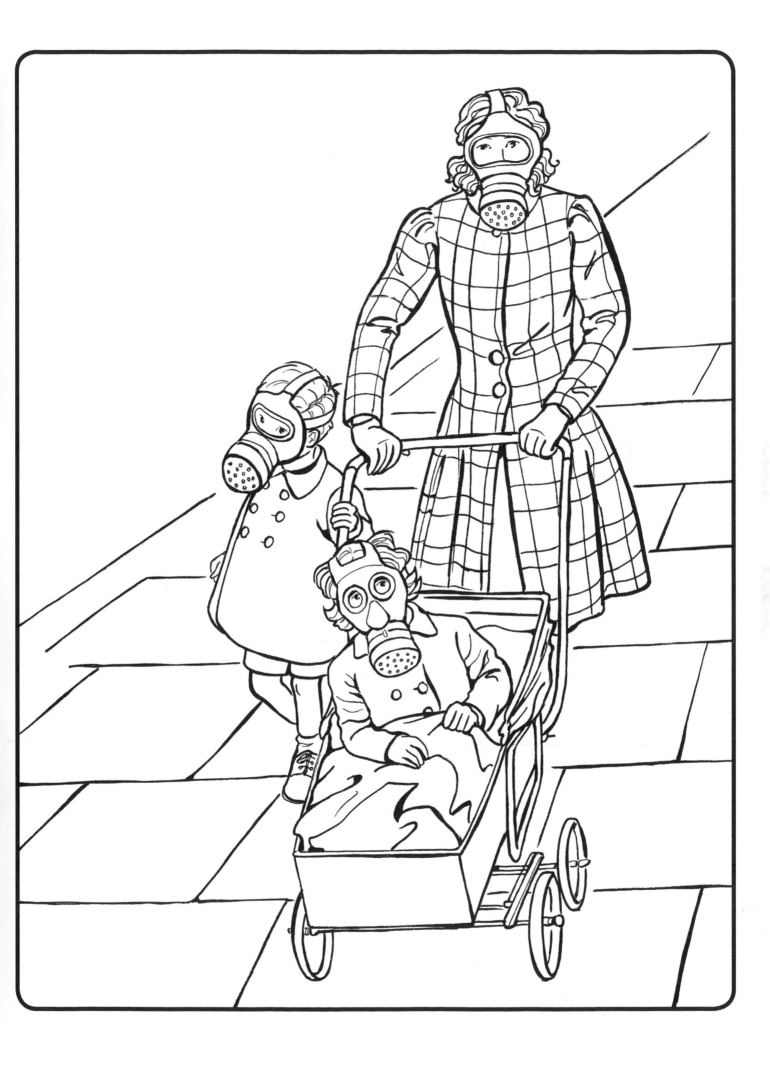

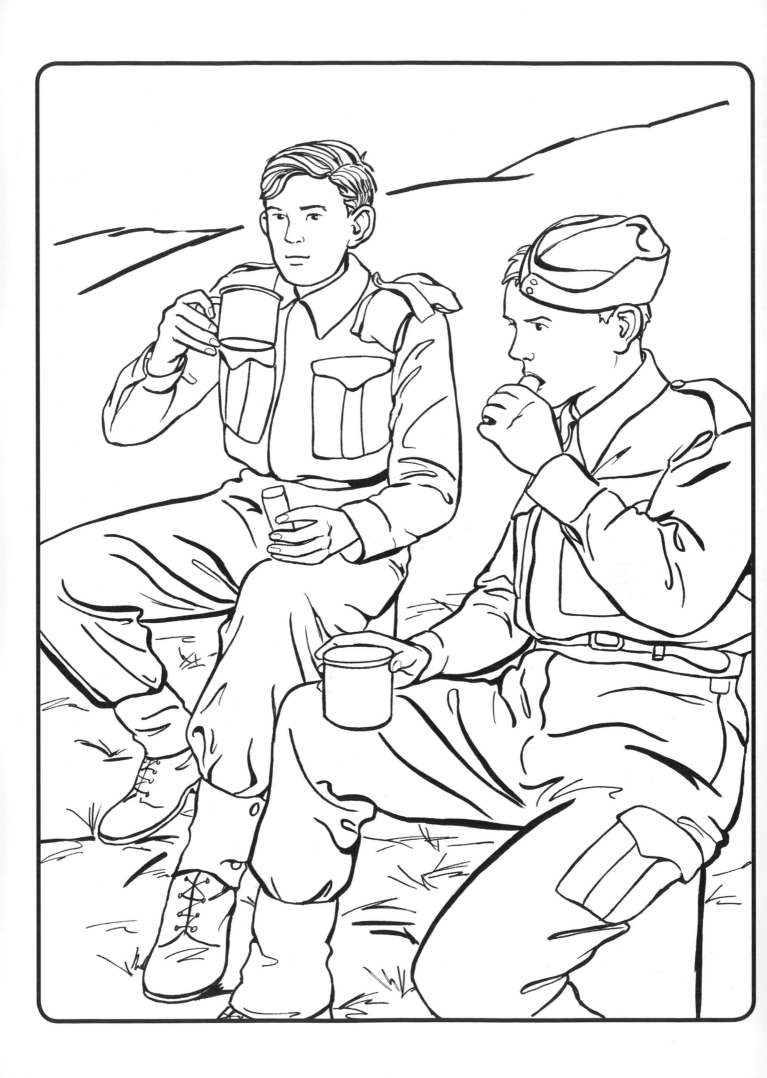

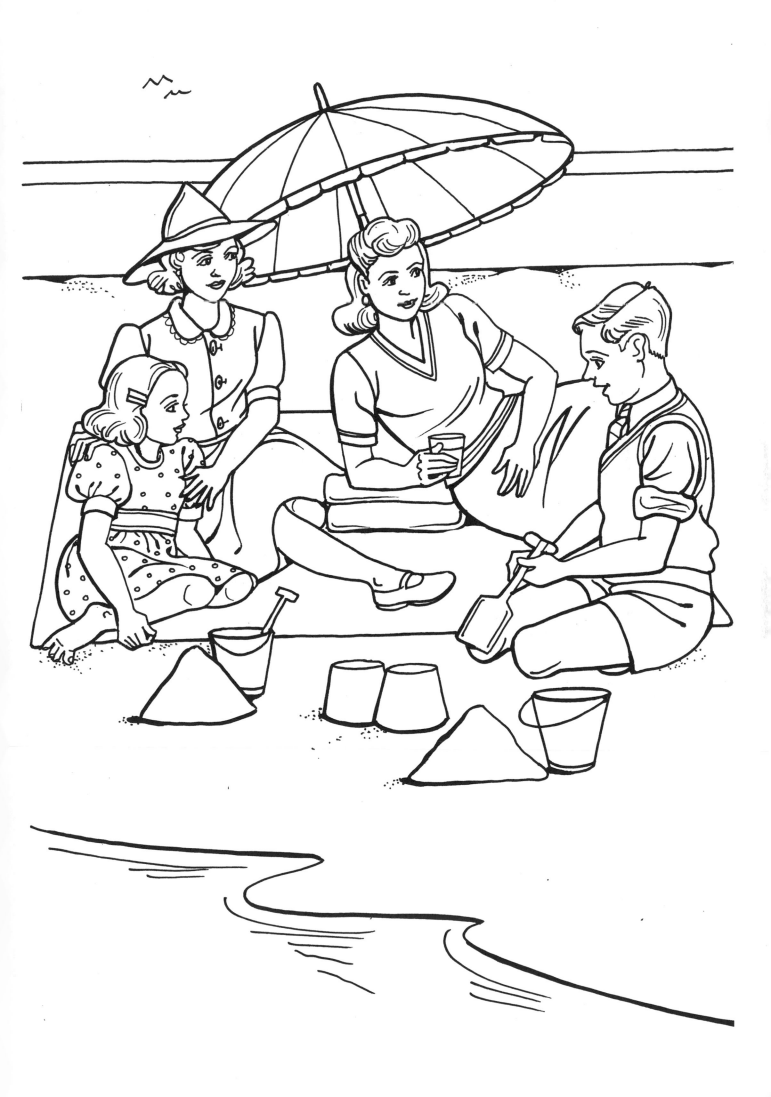

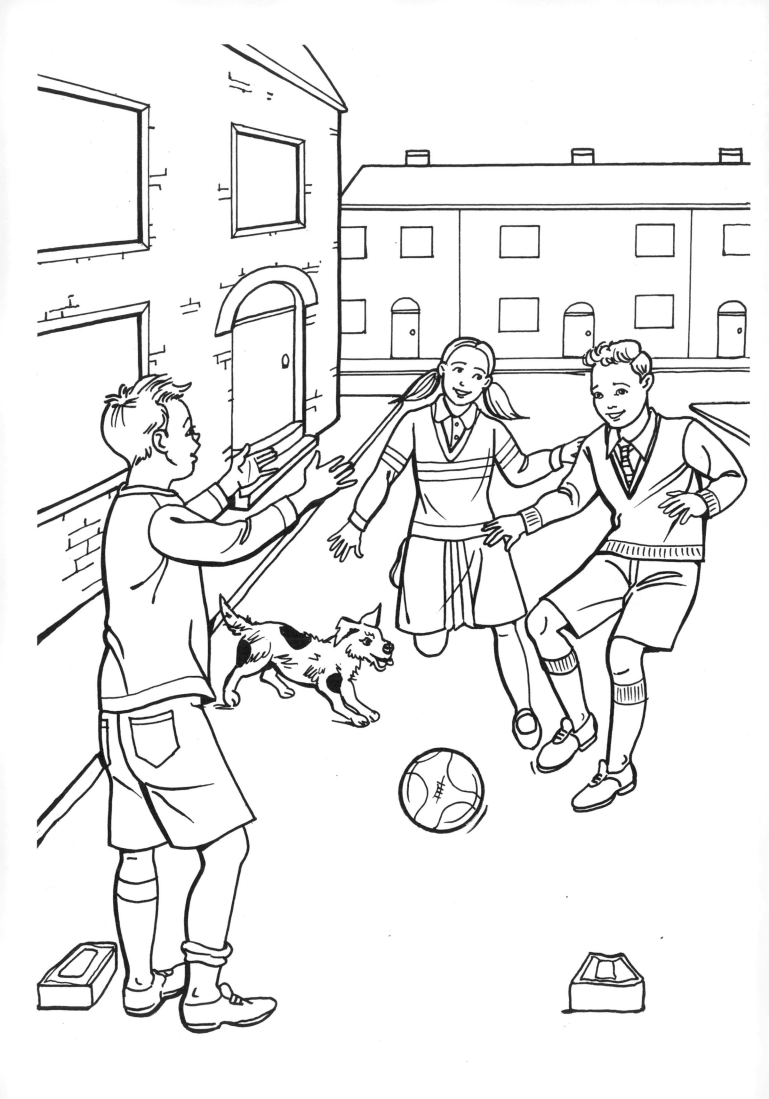

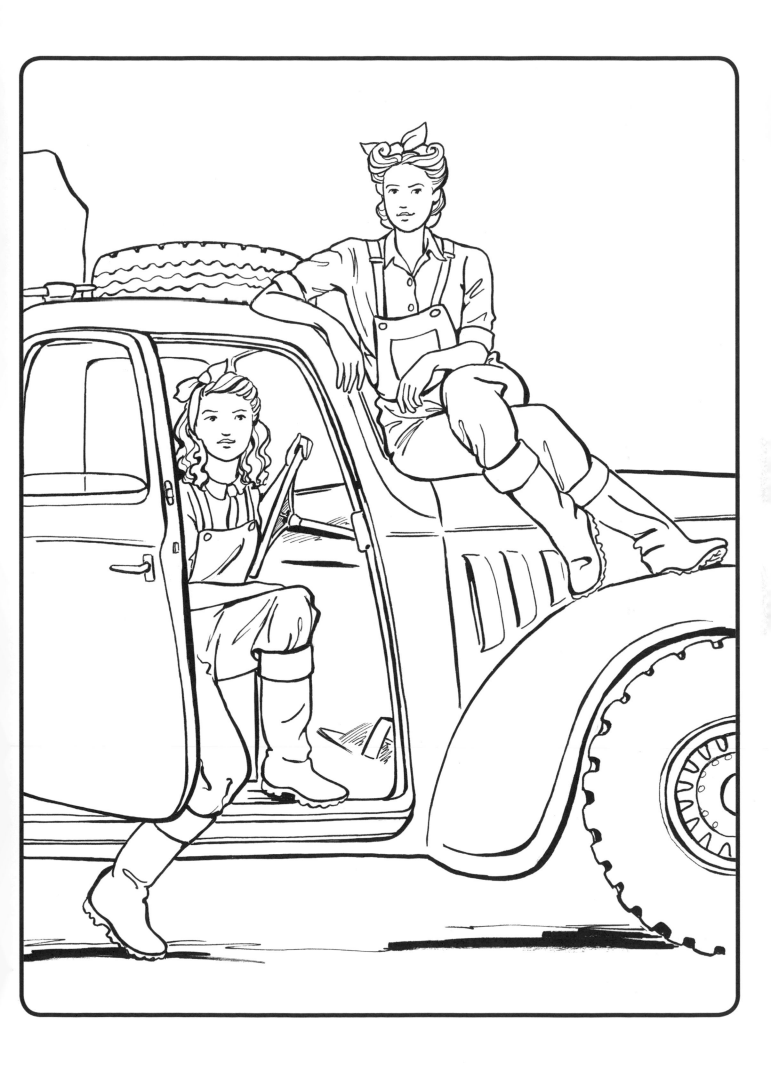

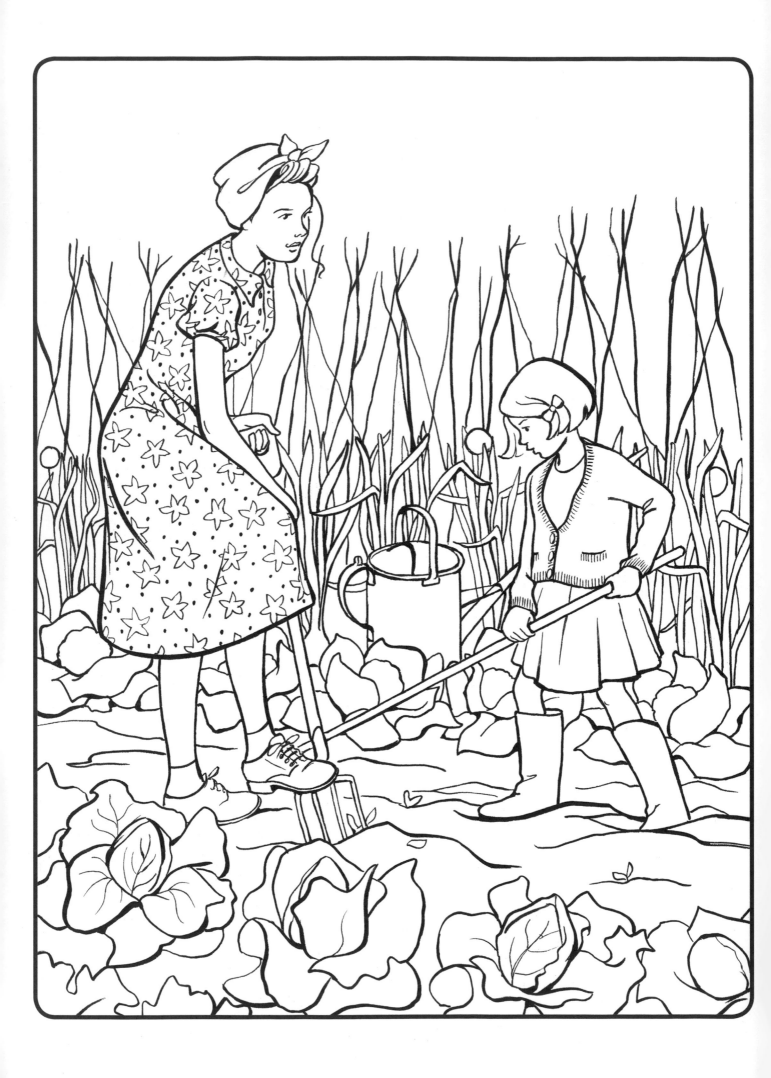

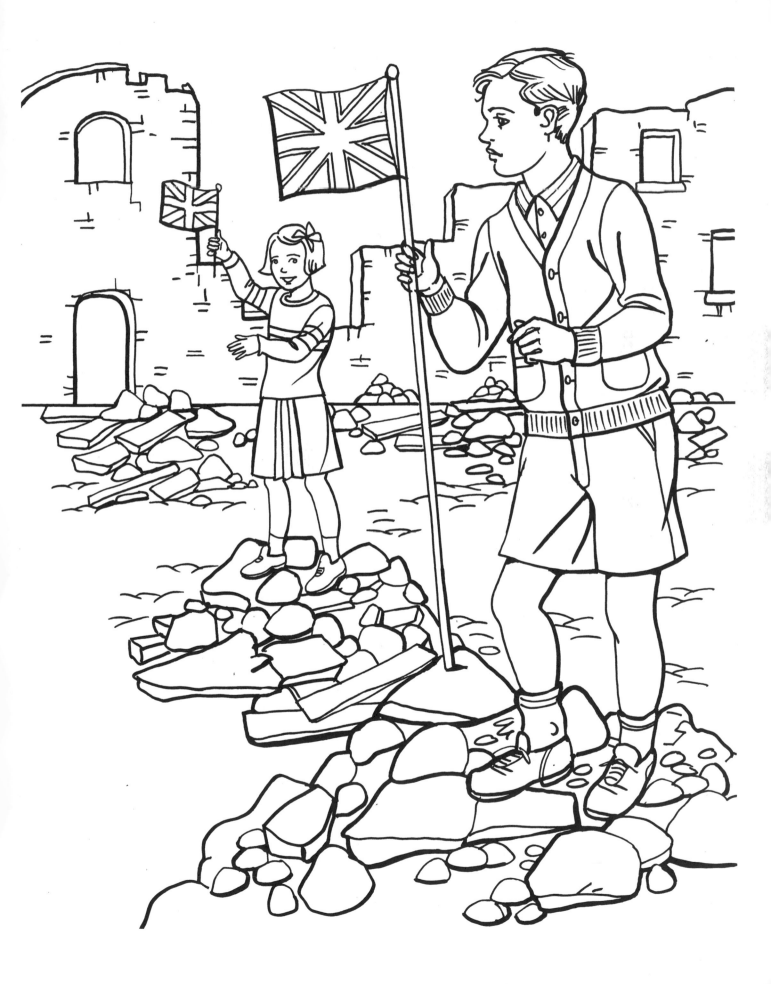

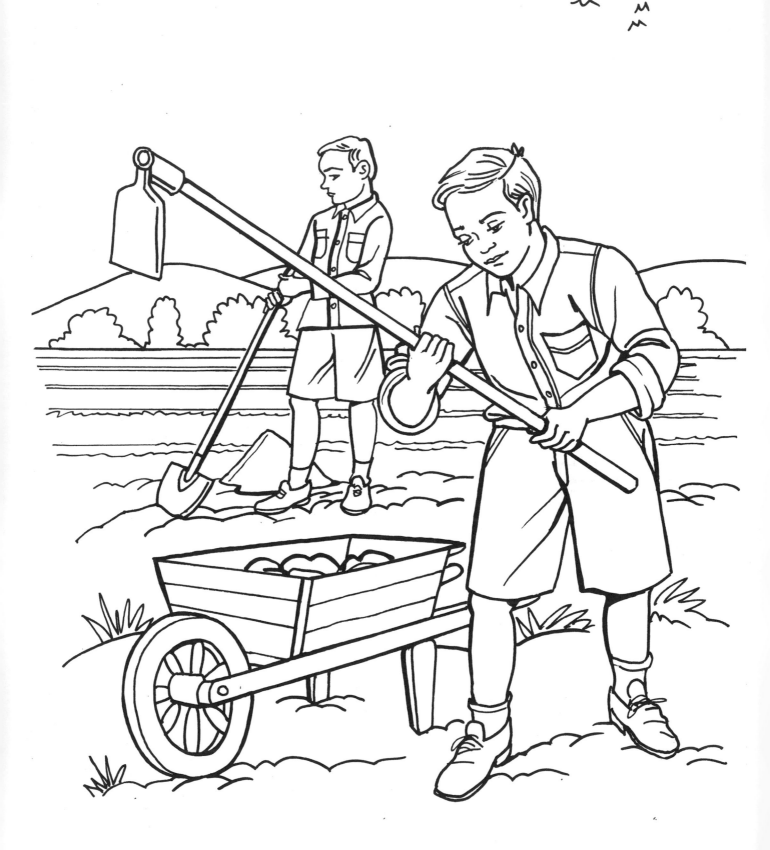

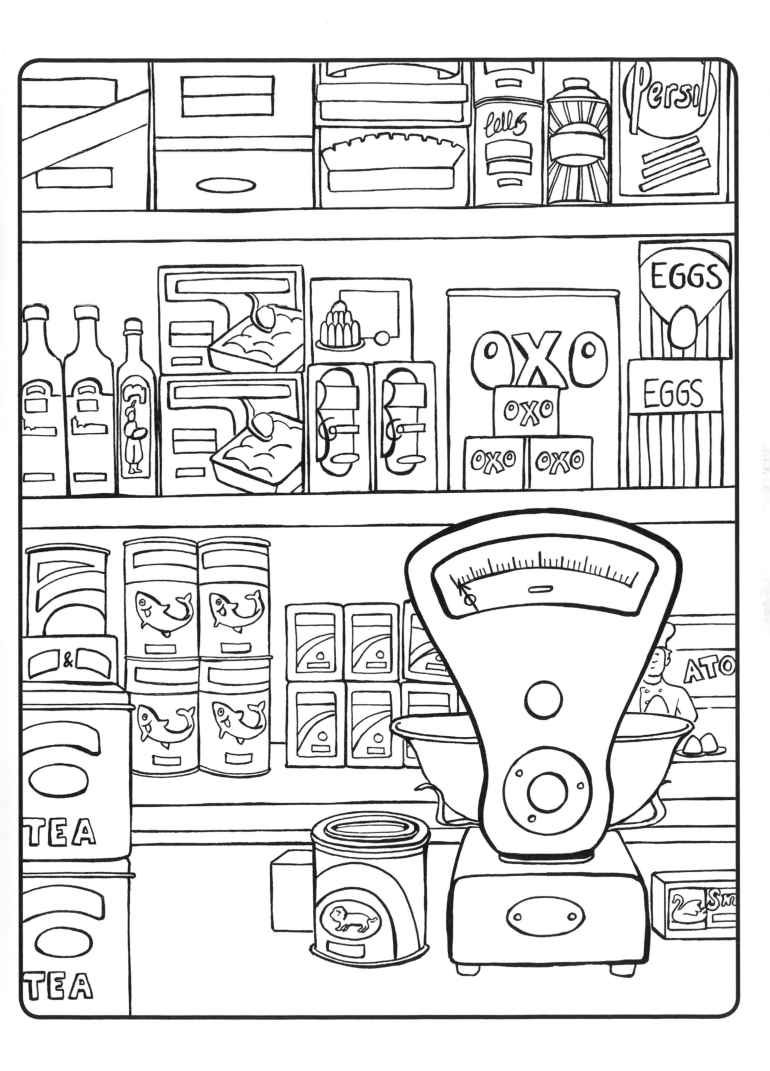

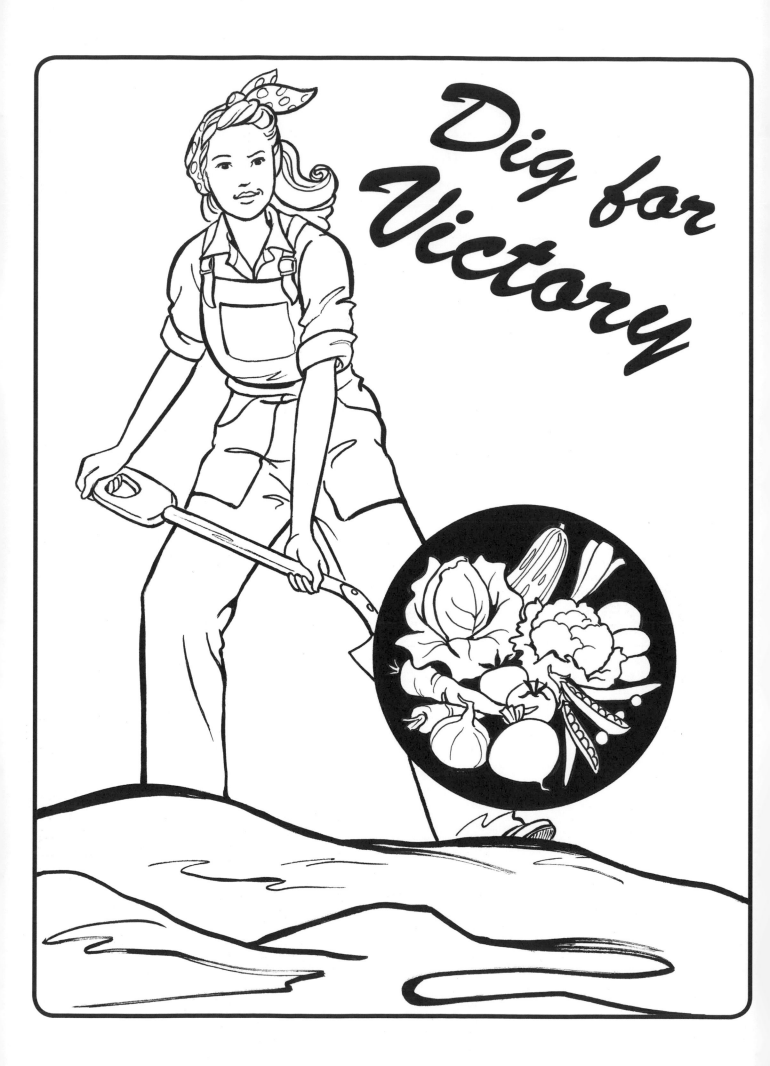

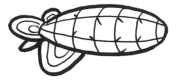
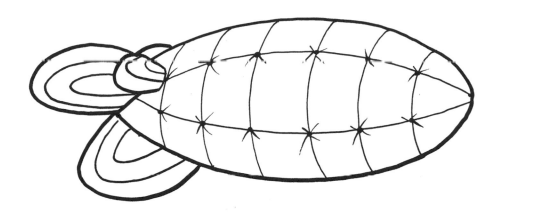
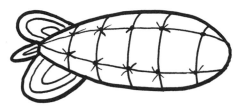
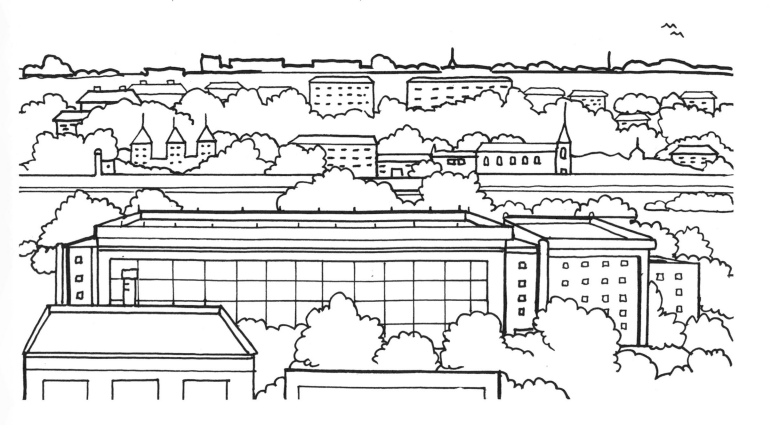

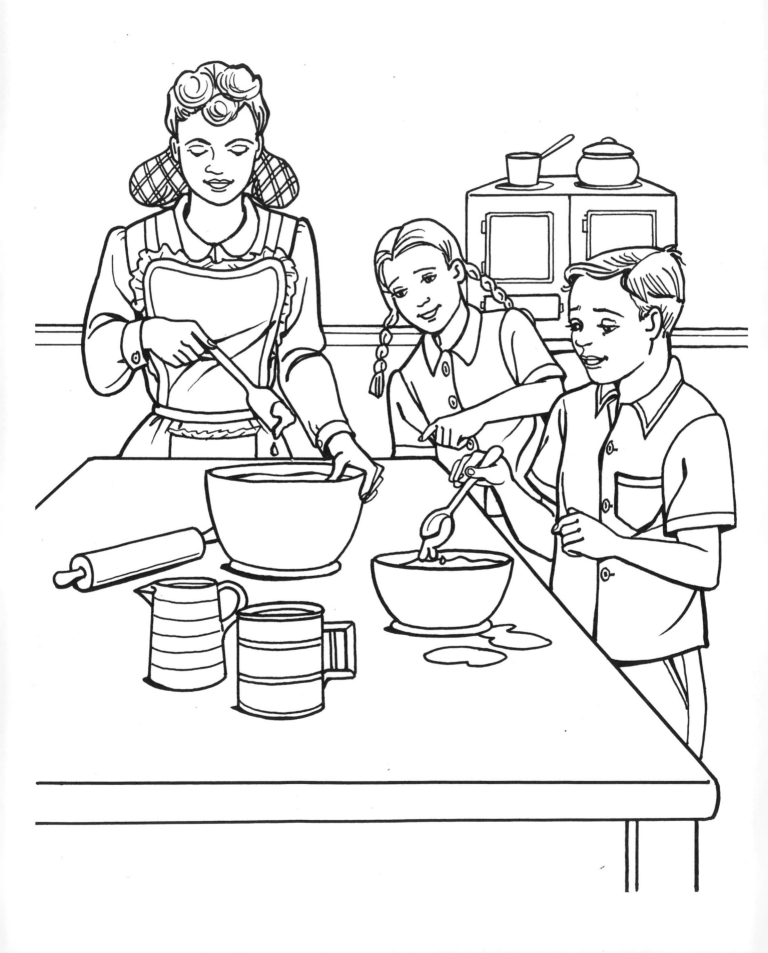

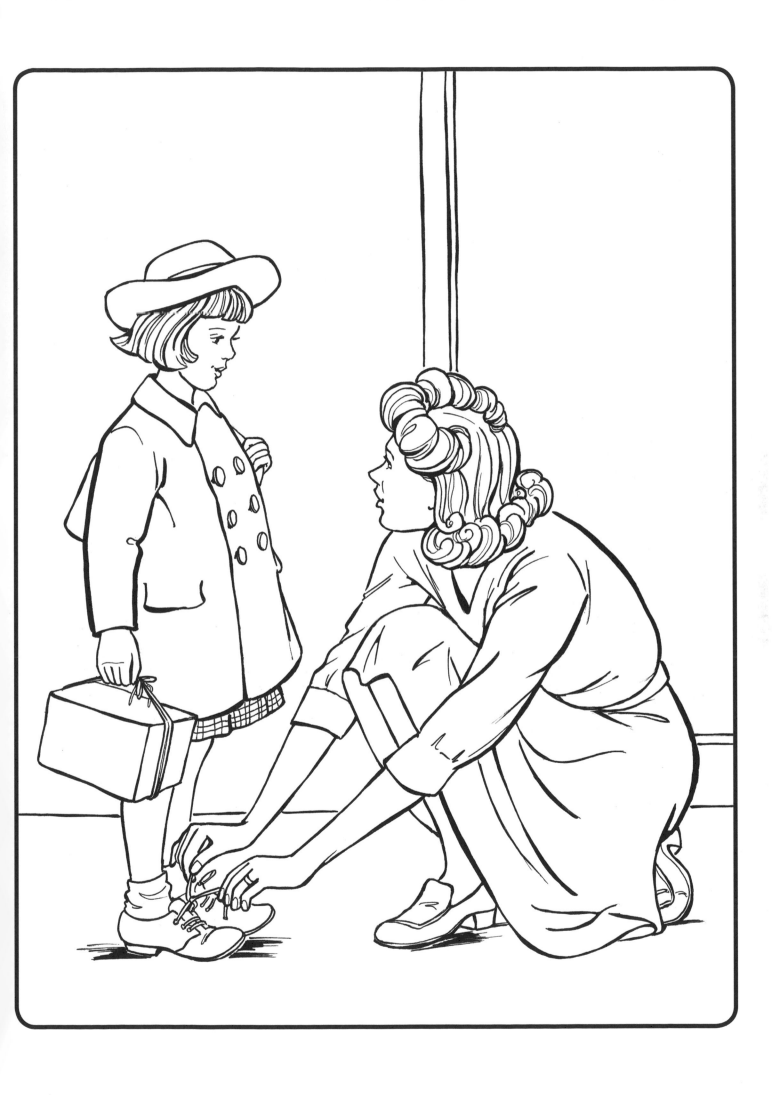

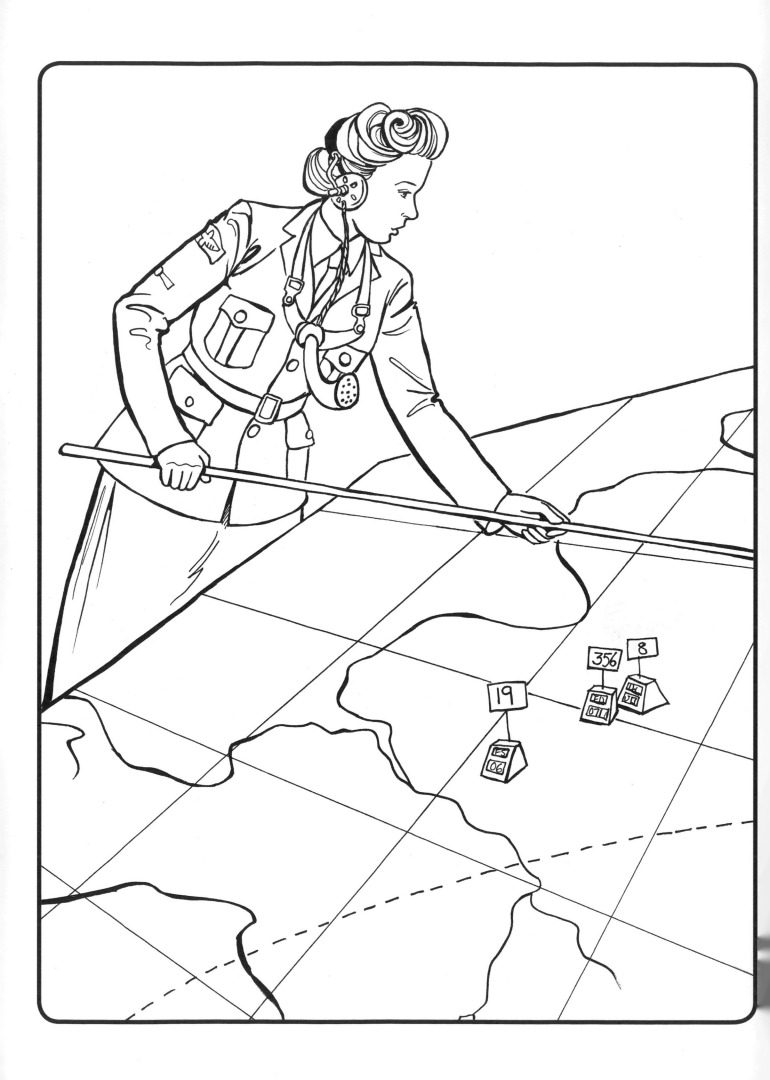

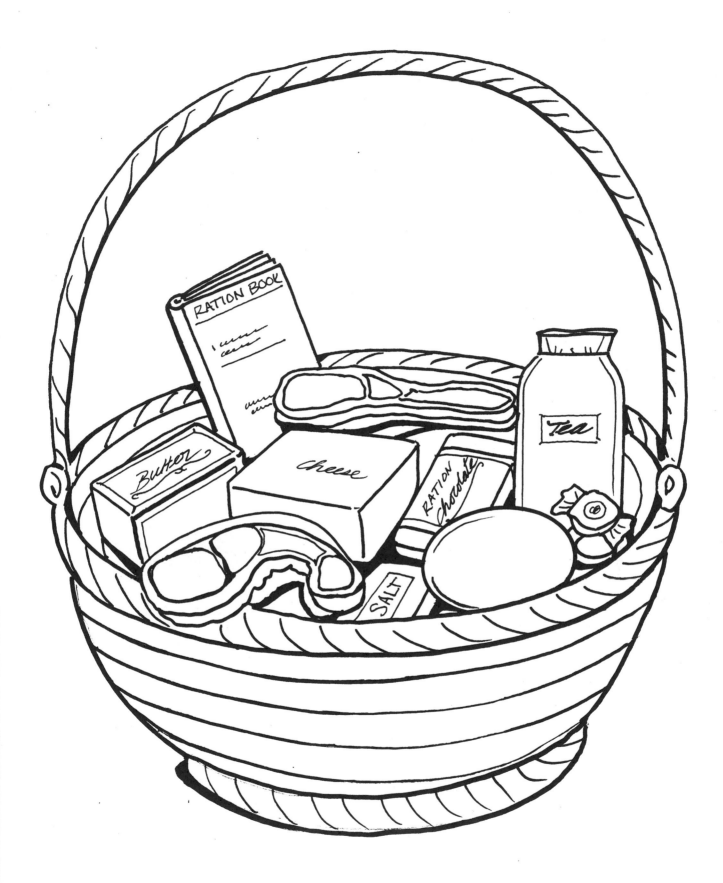

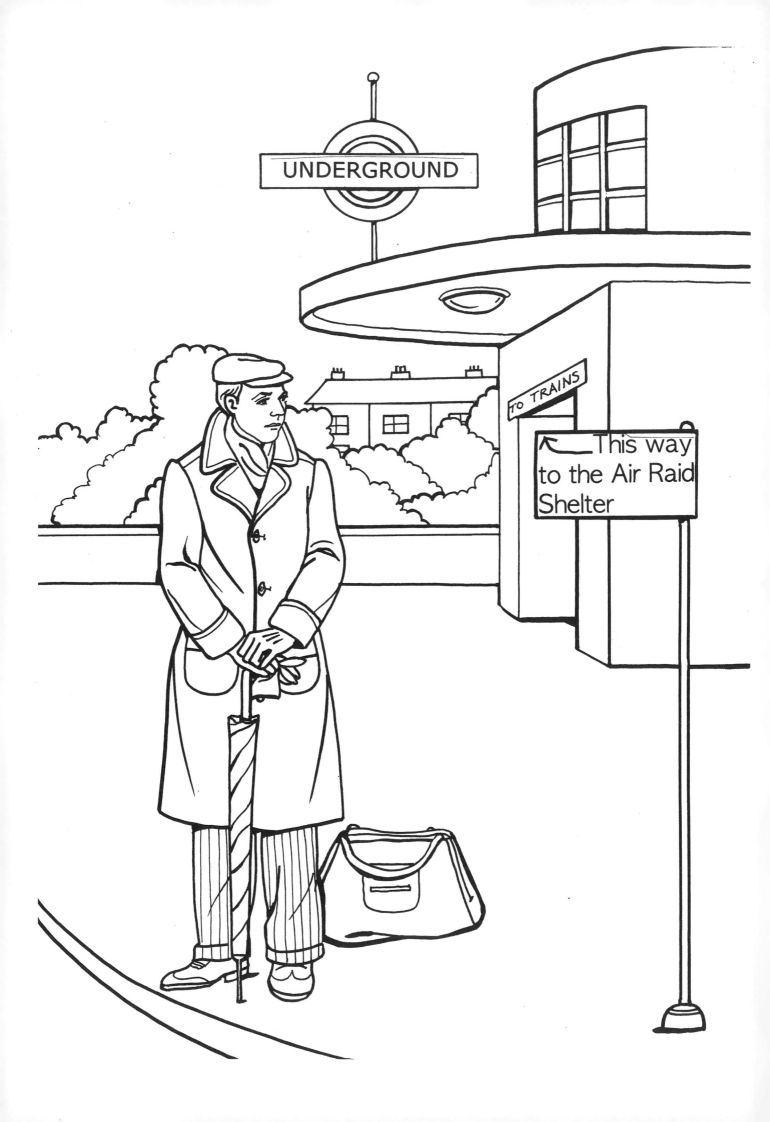

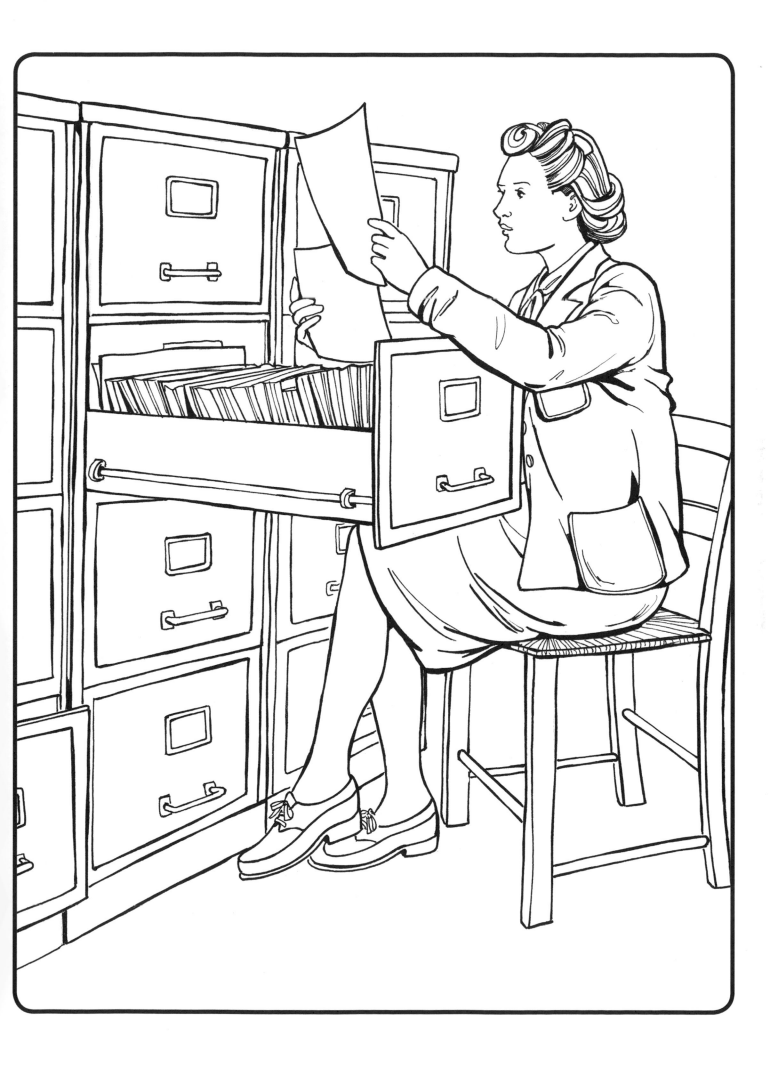

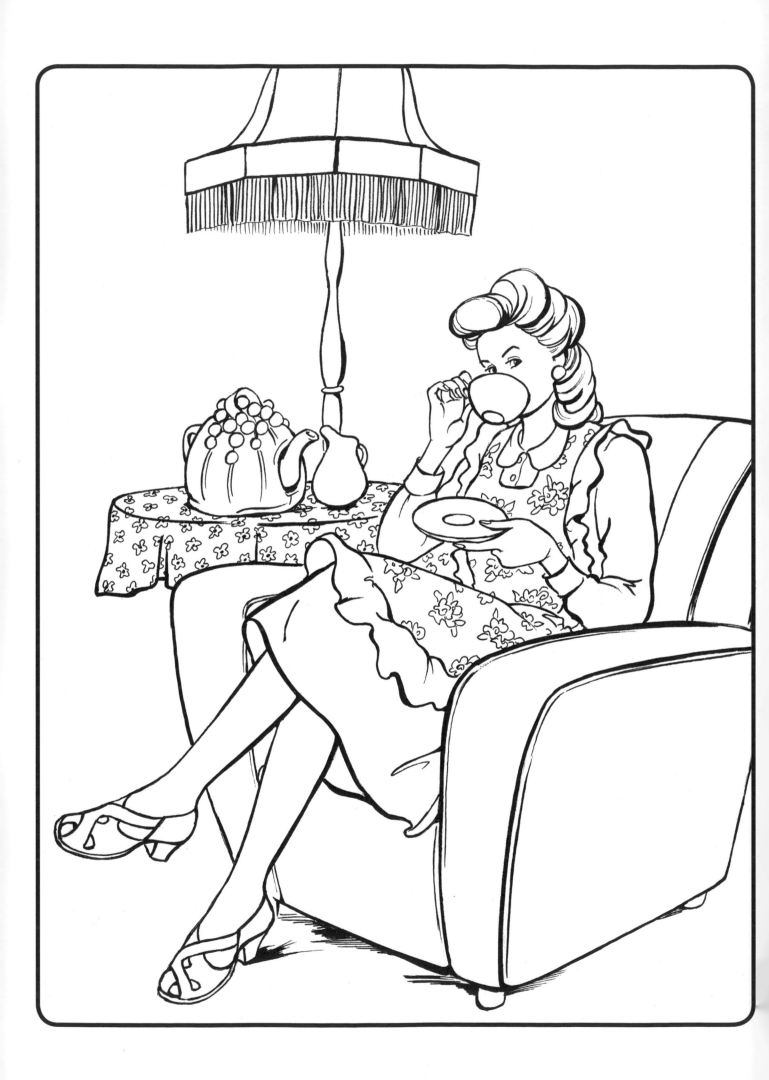

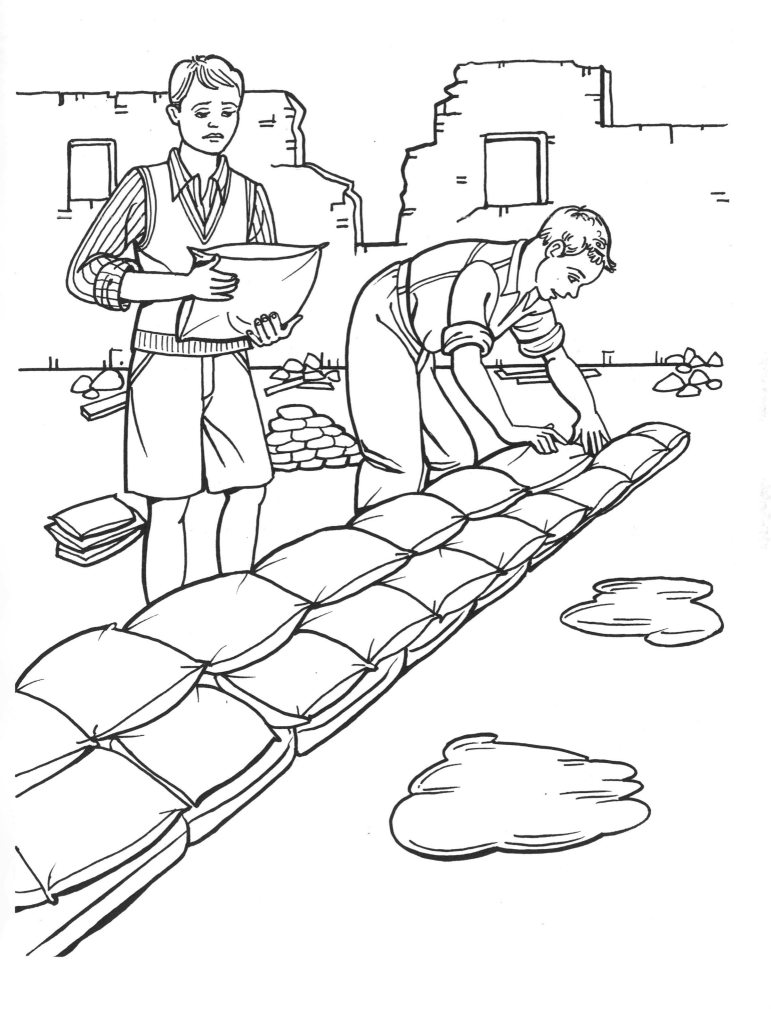

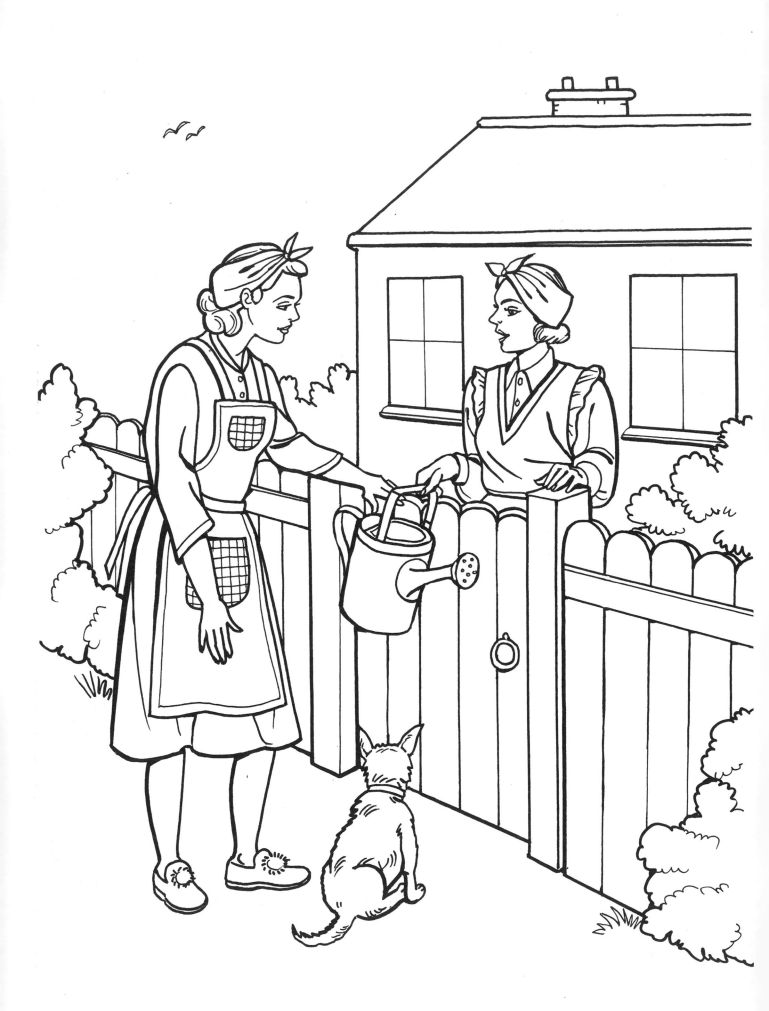

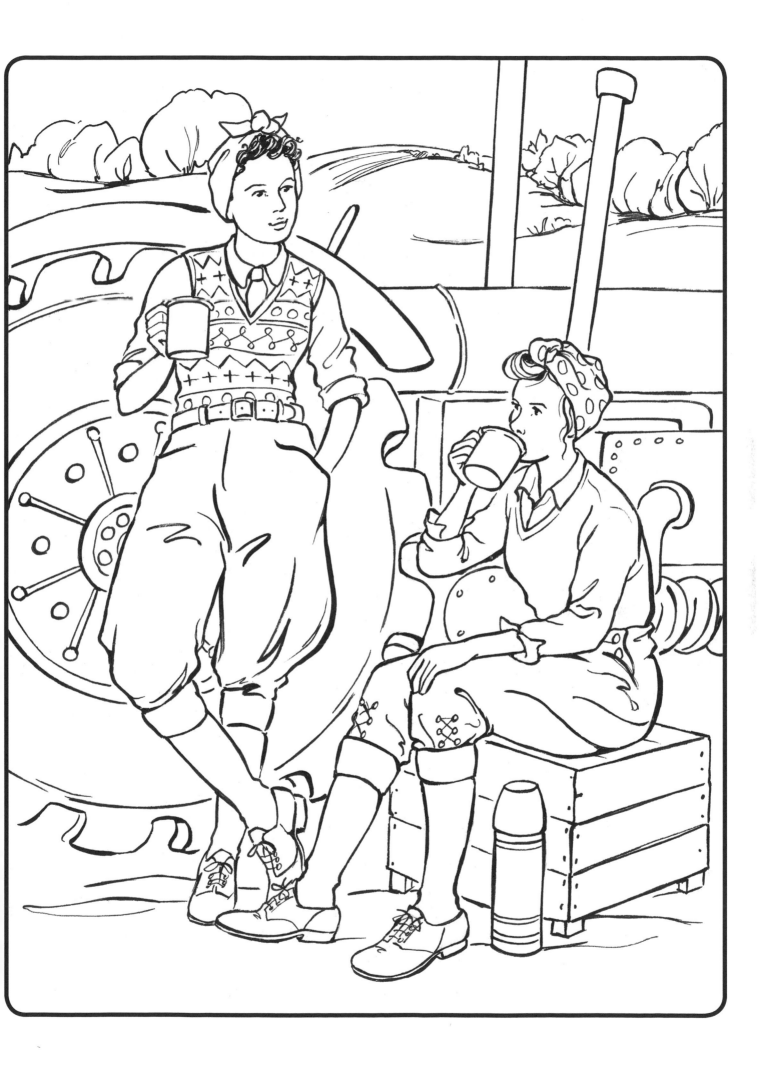

Go through your wardrobe

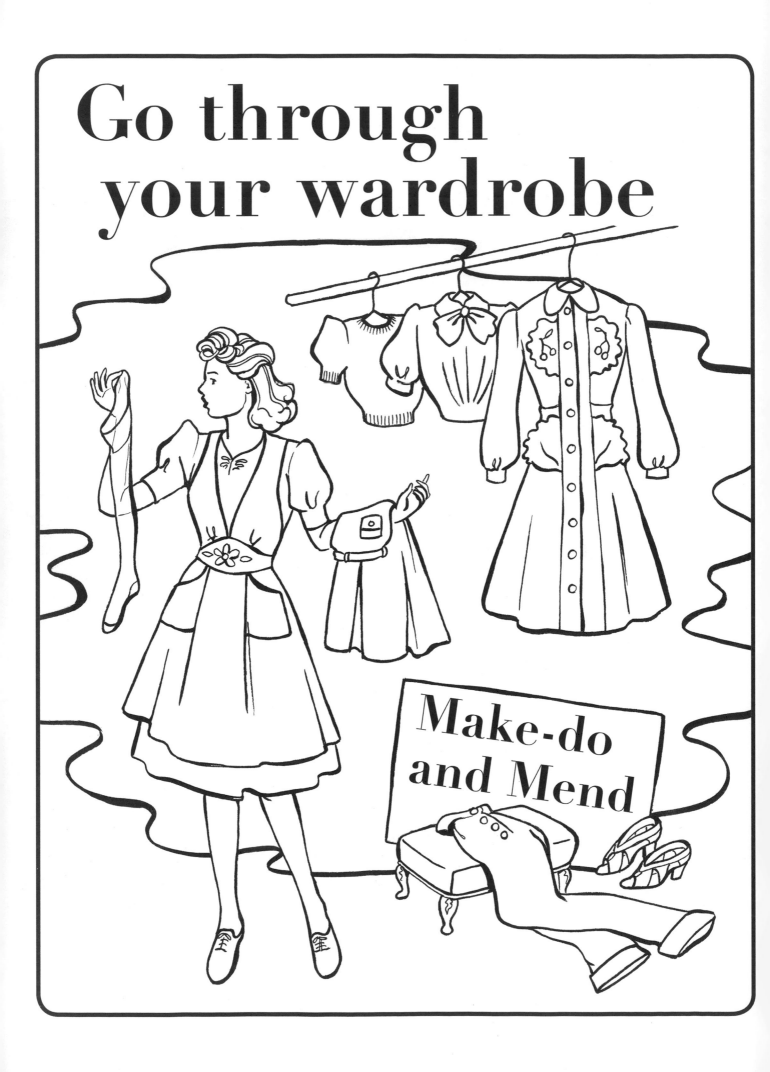

Make-do and Mend

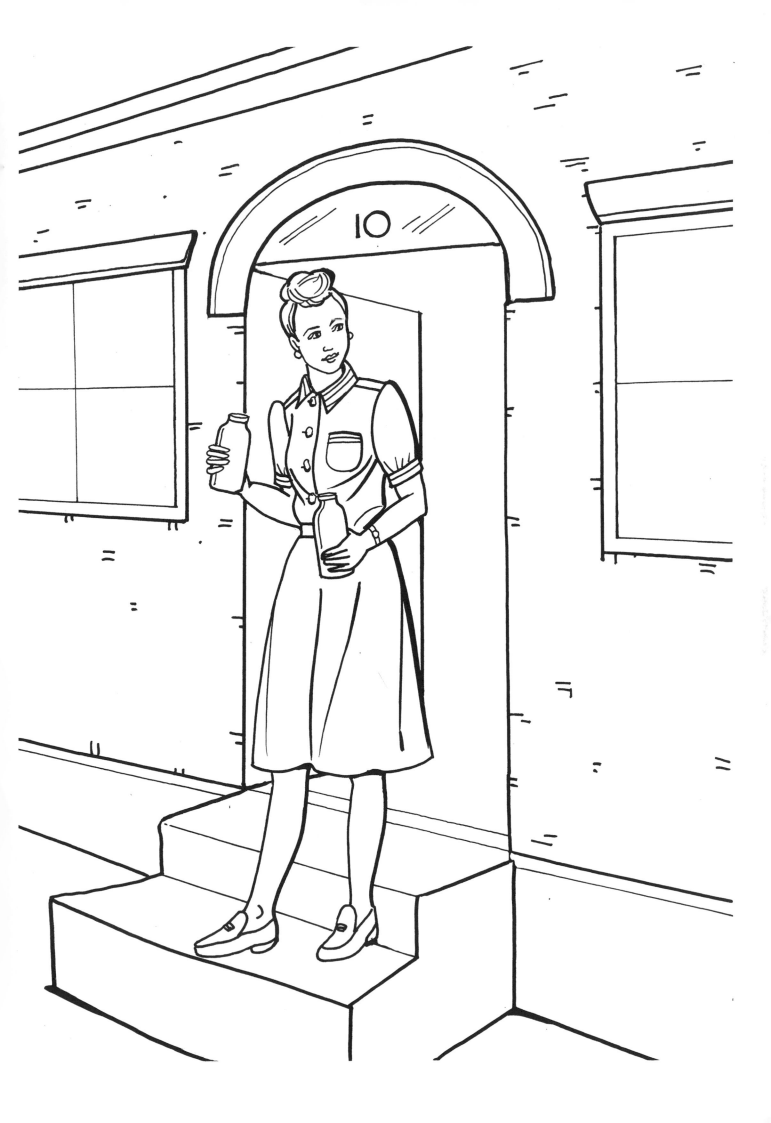

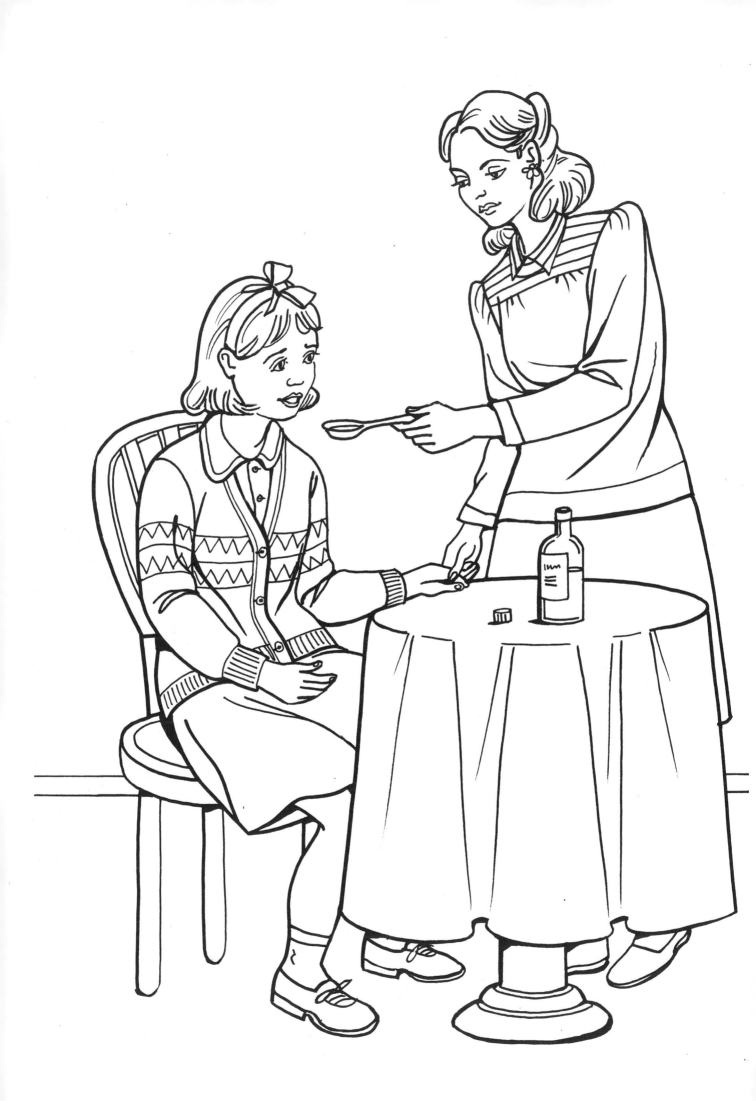

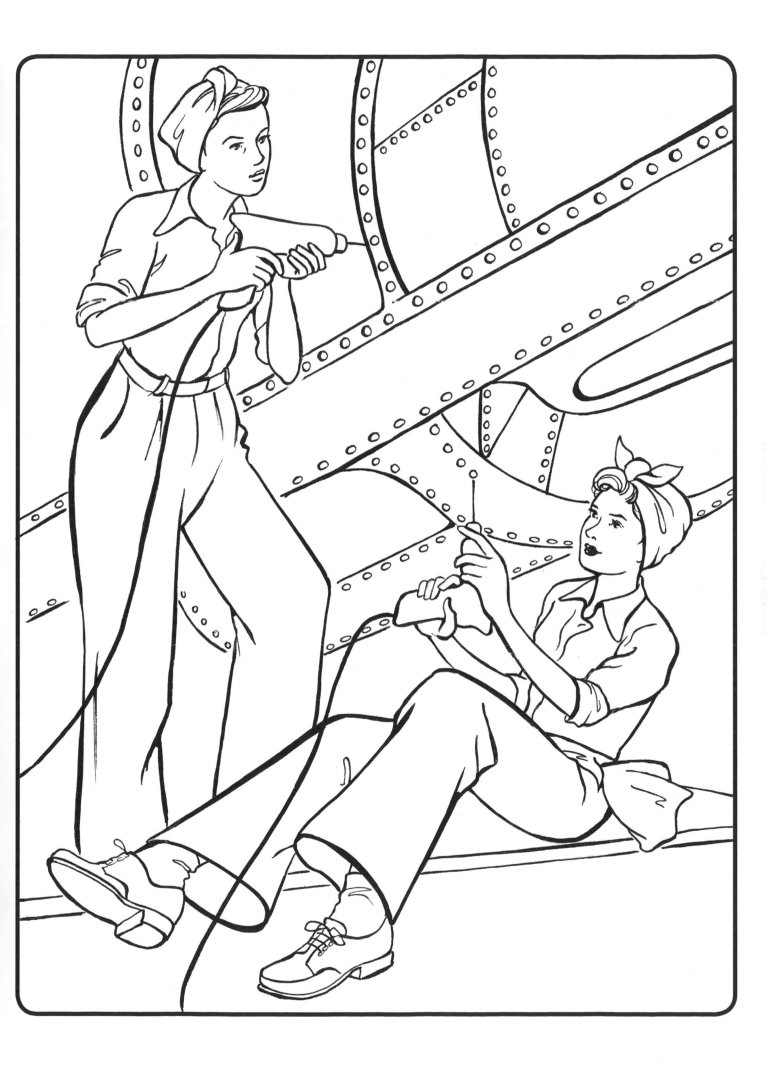

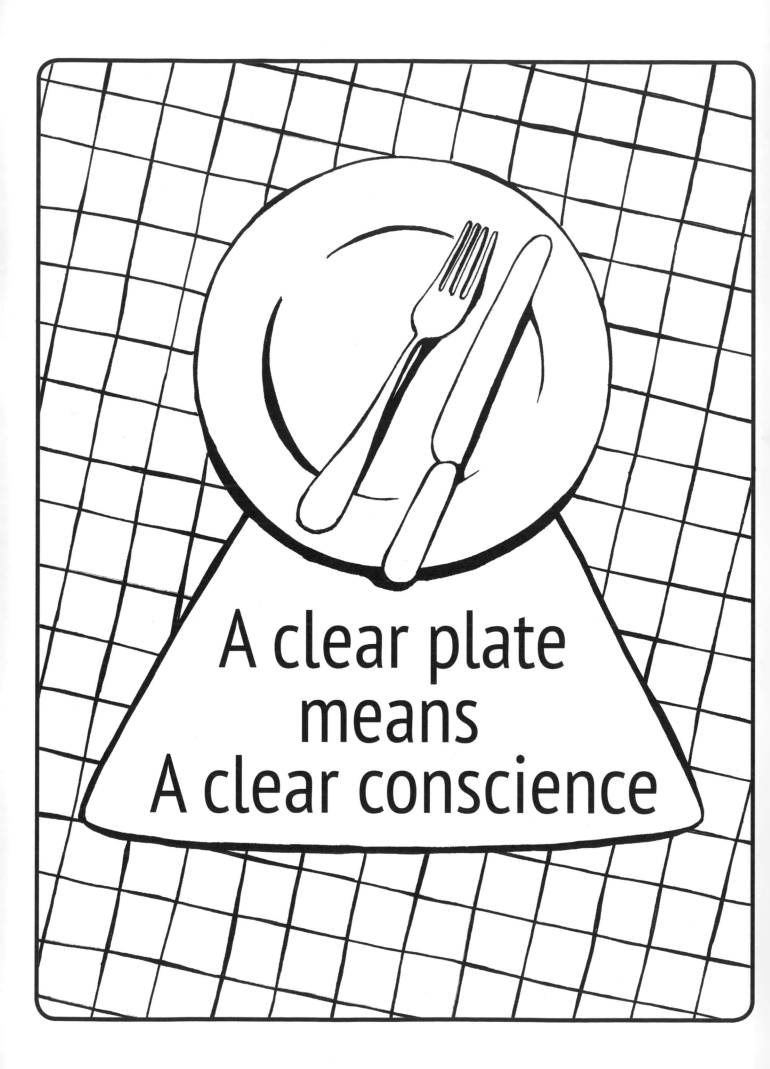

A clear plate
means
A clear conscience

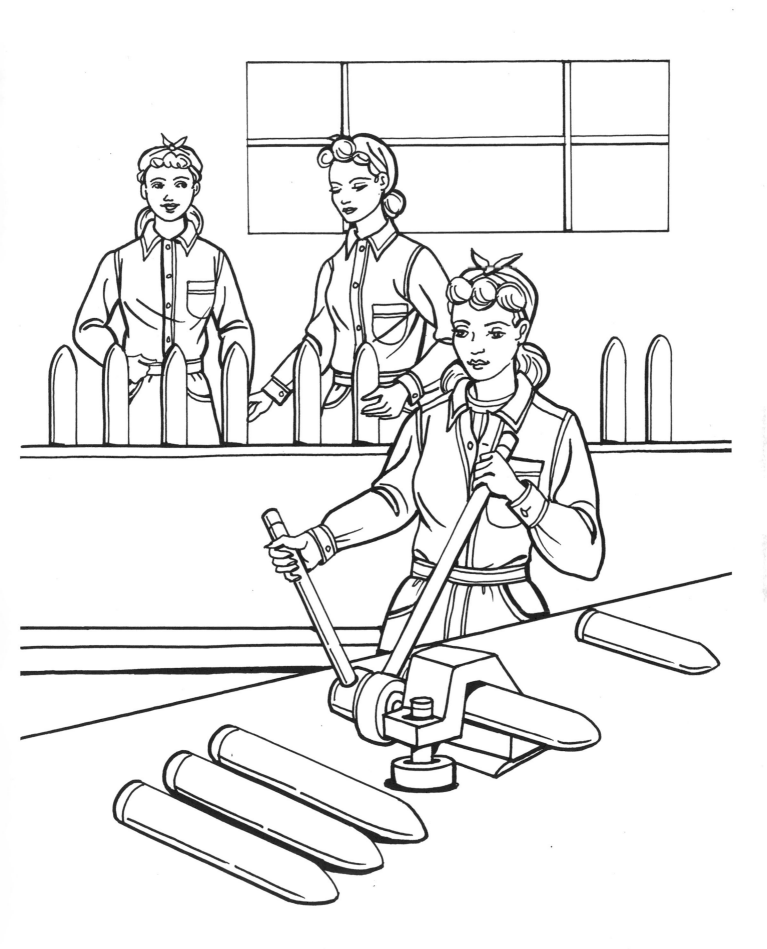

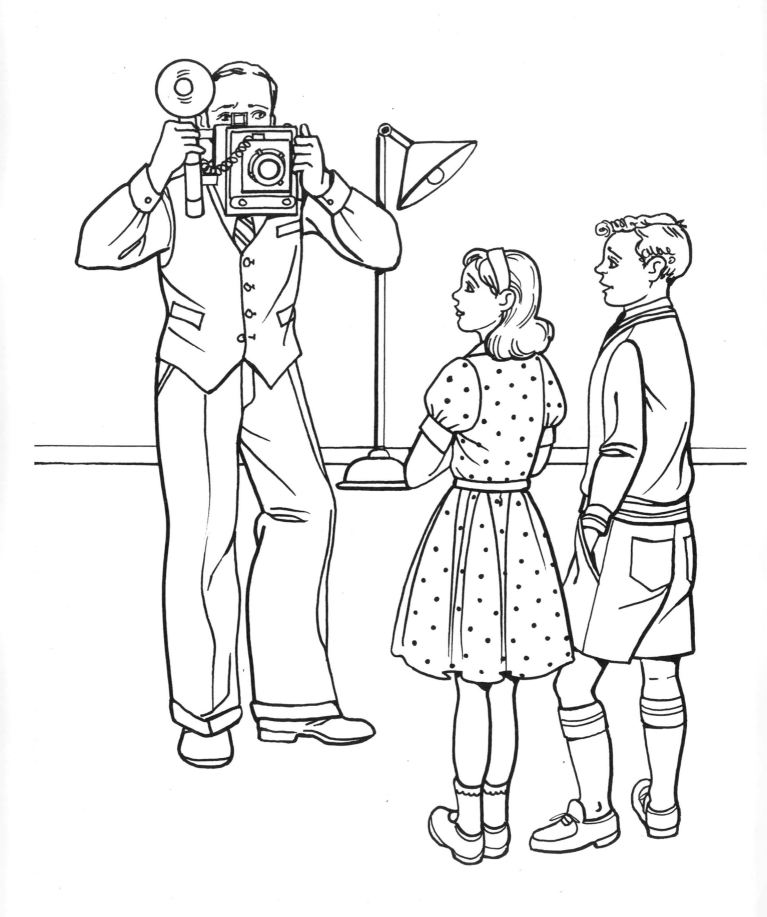

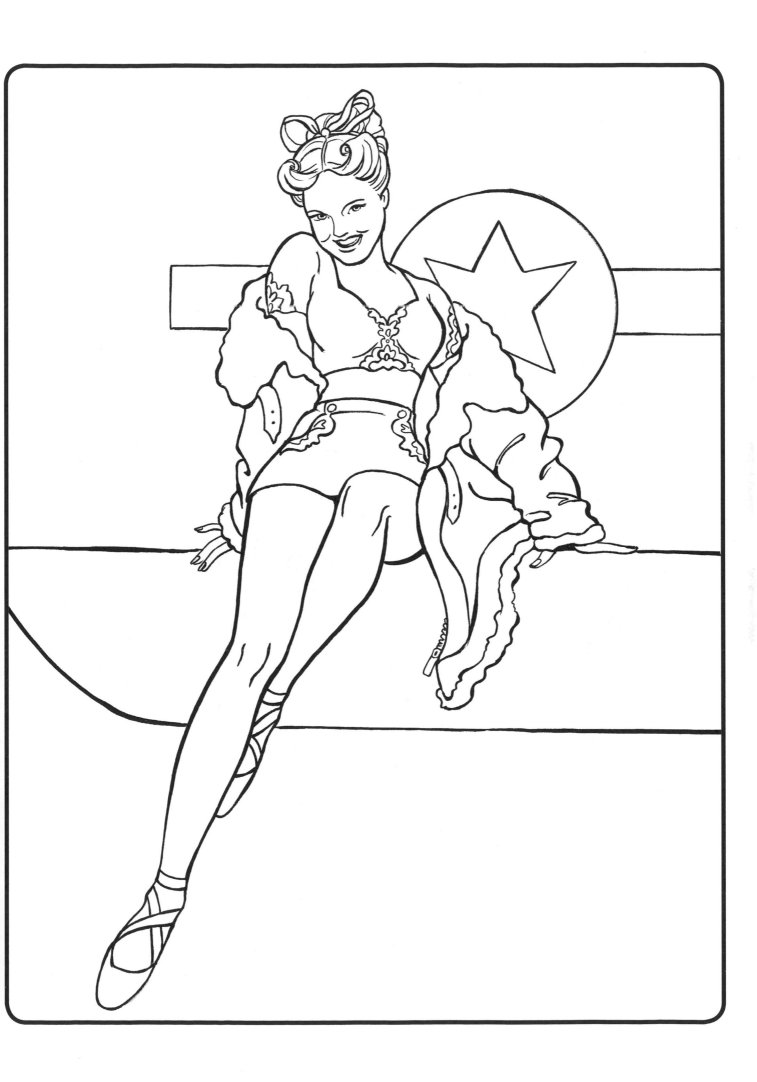

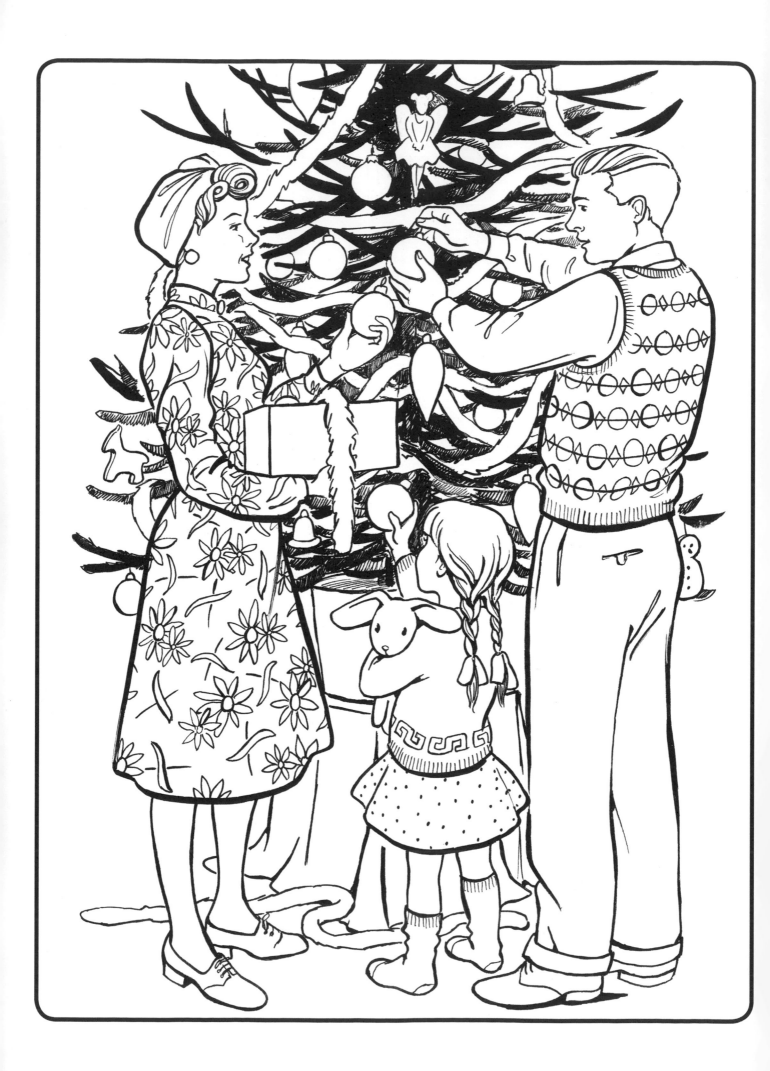

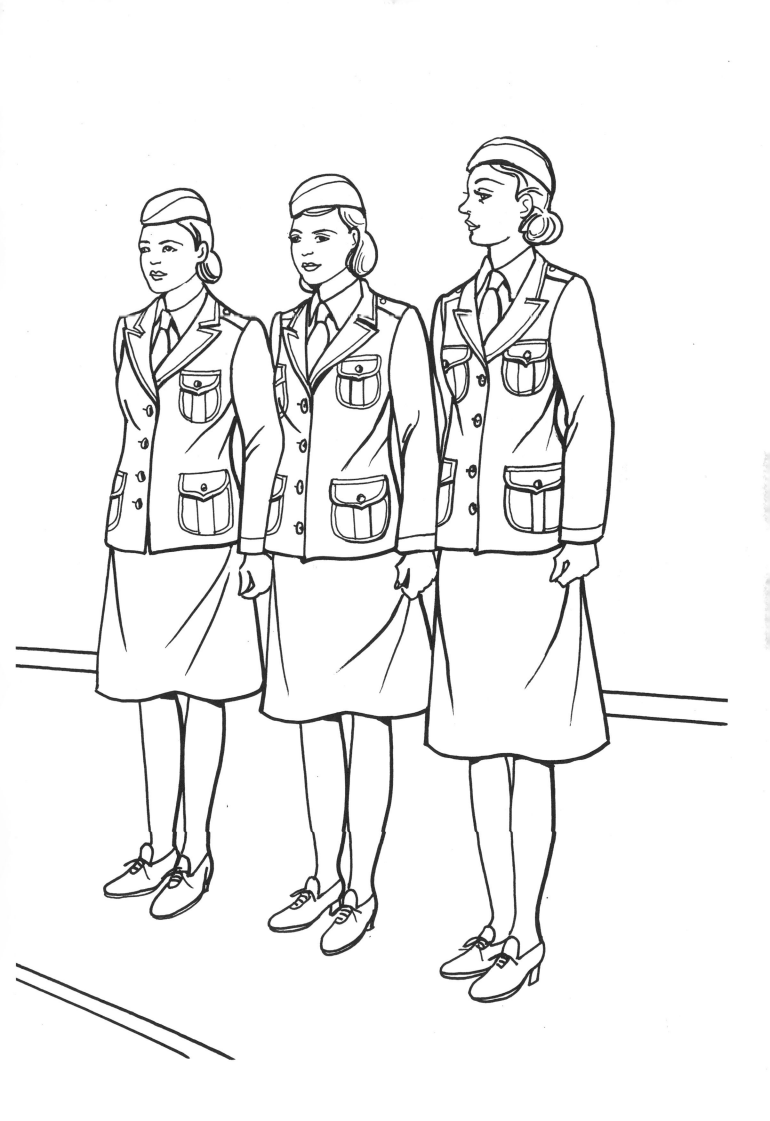

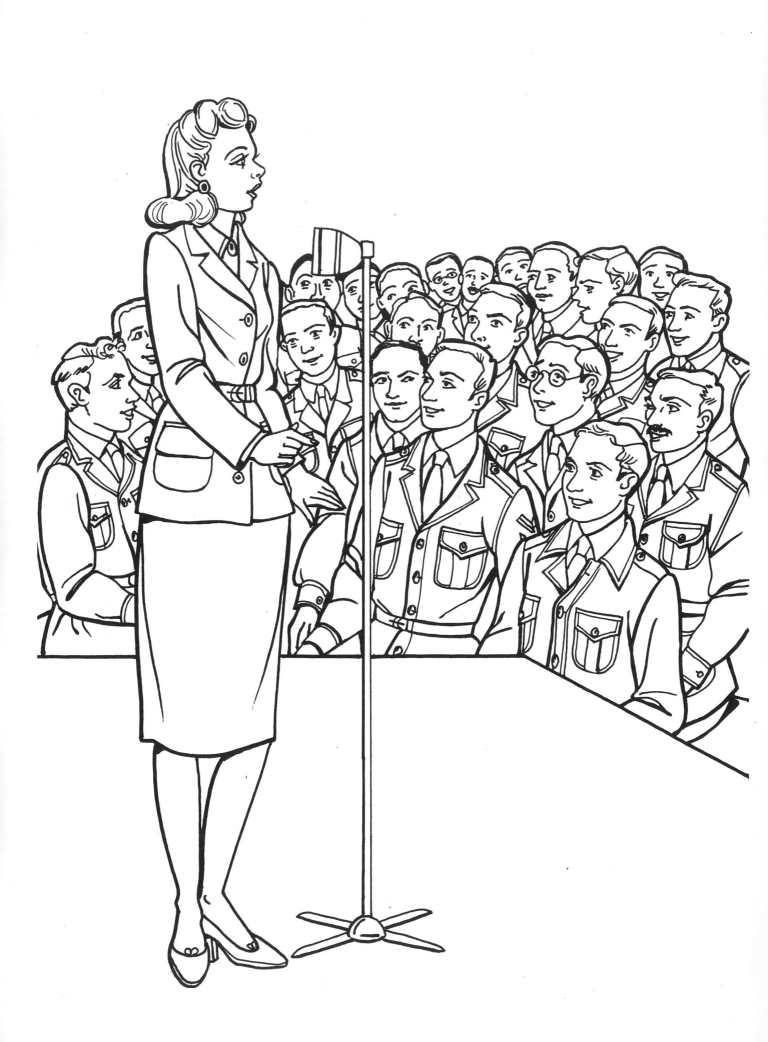

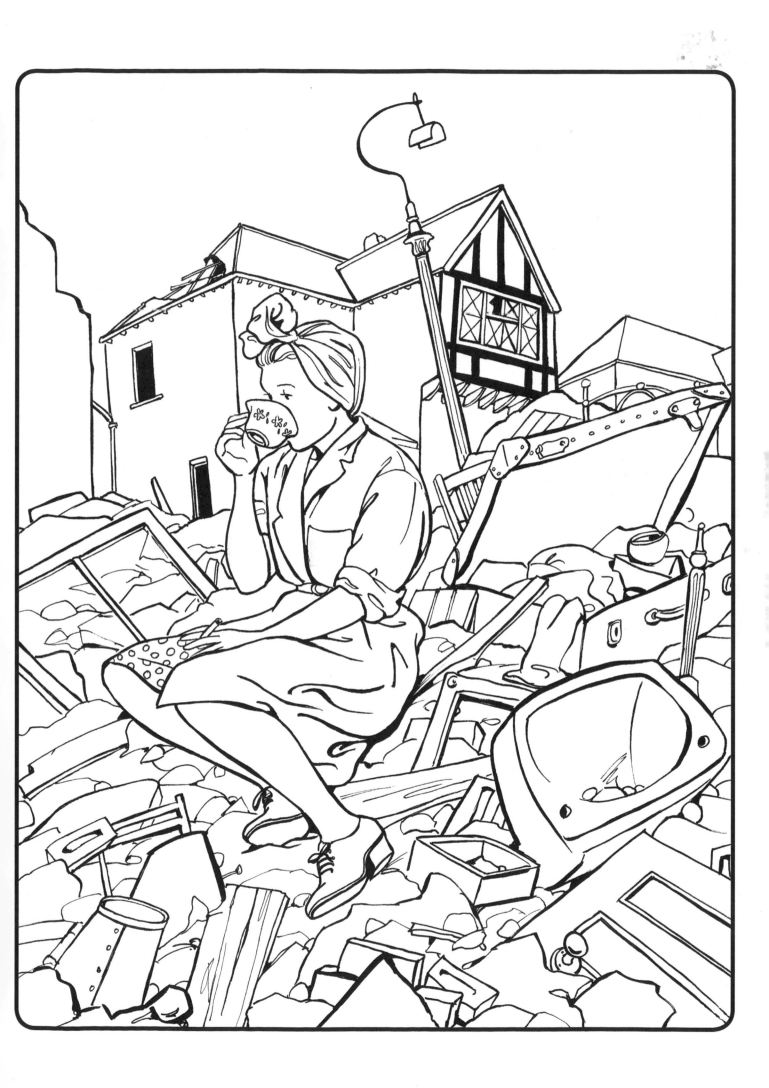

Please pack parcels

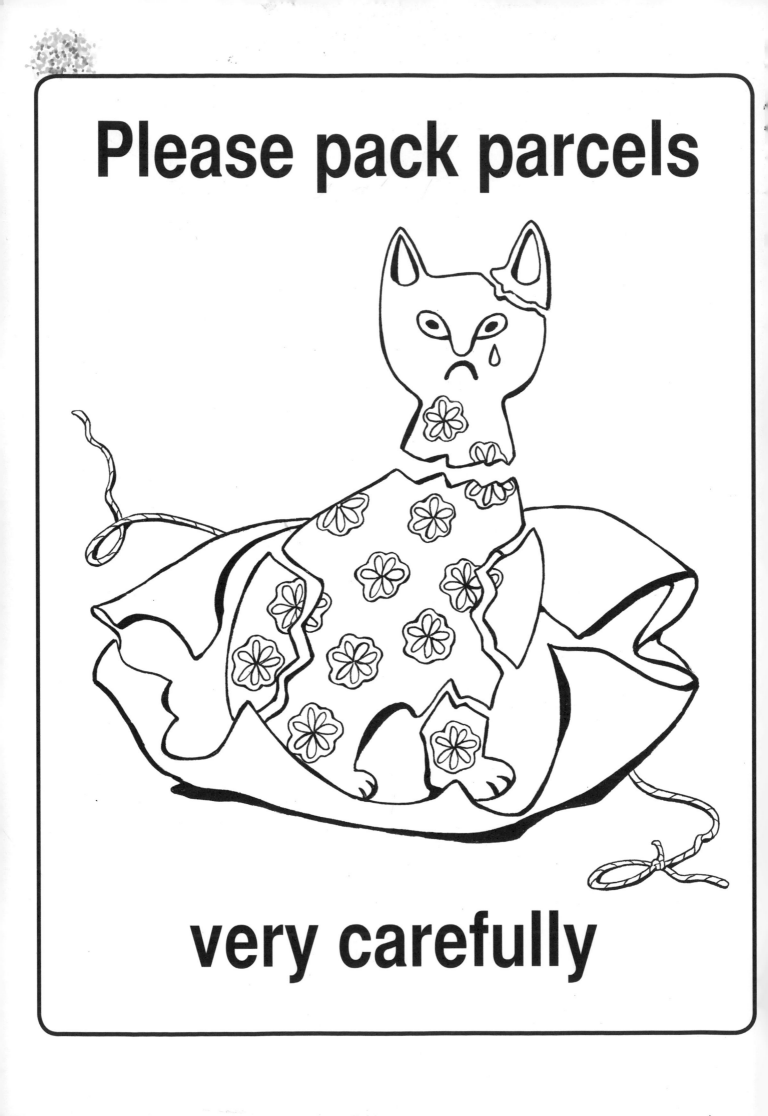

very carefully